light-duty vehicle used mainly for checking hog traps and for general transportation.

The Elk Calf: Chevrolet S-10 4x4 pickup with a small engine. A light-duty vehicle used mainly to track and locate elk and for general transportation.

Kim's Truck: Ford Explorer 4x4 SUV with a 6-cylinder engine. It was used for general transportation and elk darting, and occasionally to pull larger trailers for boats. Although this vehicle was sometimes jokingly referred to as the *grocery gitter*, it was Kim's favorite. It earned respect when used to rescue researchers and wildlife handlers after a sudden blizzard in Cataloochee, North Carolina when other vehicles got stuck in the deep snow.

BEAR IN THE BACK SEAT II

Adventures of a Wildlife Ranger
in the Great Smoky Mountains National Park

BY

Kim DeLozier &
Carolyn Jourdan

Printed in the United States of America

ISBN-13: 978-0-9885643-7-4 Softcover

Designed by Karen Key

Cover photo by Bill Lea
www.BillLea.com

CONTENTS

In this book Smoky Mountain dialect is rendered as it is actually spoken. Appalachian speech is poetic and musical. It is sung as much as spoken, so a great part of the meaning is conveyed in the cadences and tones.

It is used in conversation by people of all levels of education and intelligence, so no apostrophes will highlight the dropped g's or word variants, as if they are errors. For the same reason, the local grammar is retained.

This was done to enable the reader to experience Smoky Mountain life and language intimately, as an insider would.

Wildlife Rangers in the Great Smoky Mountains National Park have developed their own special nomenclature for referring to Park vehicles. These animal nicknames, attributed to Ranger Rick Varner, are based on the size and power of the various trucks.

The Boar: Half-ton 4x4 Dodge pickup with an 8-cylinder engine. It has a winch mounted in the bed to pull cages and traps into the back. This was the most powerful truck. It's the one used to pull the elk trailer or move bear traps that had to be transported in the bed of a truck.

The Sow: Half-ton 4x4 Chevrolet extended cab pickup with a 6-cylinder engine. It has an 8' bed which made the truck difficult to maneuver in tight places. It was good for hauling people when conducting deer counts in Cades Cove. It was big, but not very tough.

The Shoat: Half-ton 4x4 Dodge pickup with a 6-cylinder engine. A medium-strength vehicle used for tasks like towing bear trap trailers or for checking hog traps.

The Piglet: Ford Ranger 4x4 pickup with a small engine. A

BEAR IN THE BACK SEAT (AGAIN)

THE GREAT SMOKY MOUNTAINS National Park was established in 1934 and soon became famous for its black bears. Unfortunately, back then, and for several decades afterwards, nobody knew how to professionally manage live black bears in the wild. In most cases, the rangers had to learn how to deal with the animals by trial and error.

Black bears aren't generally as aggressive as grizzly bears or polar bears, but they're unbelievably strong and smart. Some studies indicate that they're more intelligent than dogs.

Was I smarter than the average bear? Not at first. For years I was on a steep learning curve in dealing with them. And the Park visitors who encounter these crafty black bruins never stand a chance in outwitting them.

During the early years, many bears that caused problems for Park visitors were simply shot. Rangers don't like to have to do this. Black bears are the icons of the Smokies and part of our job is to protect them. We enjoy them as much as tourists do. So, instead of simply killing them, we decided to experiment with moving nuisance bears away from the populated areas.

This worked very well. We learned that if we took the bears deeper into the woods, they were usually able to live out their lives in the wild without causing any further problems. Some years we moved dozens of bears. Then gradually we realized that it wasn't really the bears' fault. We were teaching them bad habits.

The origin of the problem was that Park visitors were leaving enormous amounts of food scraps out where the bears could get to them. It's very easy for the bears to find garbage because they have what many scientists believe is *the most sensitive nose in the world.*

Their sense of smell is seven times better than a bloodhound's and 2,100 times better than a human's. They can smell food from a great distance. With so many visitors grilling and frying hamburgers, hotdogs, and chicken throughout the Park, bears don't need a GPS to find an easy and tasty meal.

So, in the days before we focused on providing bear-proof trash-cans to lock up the food the scraps, I handled wild black bears frequently. One of my most memorable lessons came when I got a report of a bear being active in the Chimneys picnic area.

In those first years I was very excited to respond to a bear call, especially if I was going to need to dart it with tranquilizing drugs. I'd grab the dart pistol and take off up the road. I thought I had to respond like I was David Hasselhoff on *Baywatch*, running to save a drowning person, but I had it all wrong.

I believed that time was of the essence in these situations, and in some cases it was. But, over the years I came to realize that a bear might leave before I arrived, but if he did, it was no big deal. If he was a real problem, he'd keep coming back. What I actually needed to do when I got a call was to stop, take a deep breath, and make a plan. Unfortunately I rarely did that.

On this particular day, as soon as I got the call, I took off in a little CJ5 Jeep instead of a truck and I didn't bother to take the time to load up an animal transfer cage. That was two bad mistakes right at the outset.

After a humbling and humiliating incident, I'd learned to be careful with the dart gun, but I was still green and didn't always take the time to get the right vehicle or bring the right equipment with me.

It was a hot summer afternoon and the smell of barbequed chick-en, hamburgers, and hotdogs filled the picnic area. The delicious smells were more than the poor bear could resist. He wanted the food more than he feared the irate families. He wasn't listening to what his momma had taught him when he was a cub.

I was lucky and I got there while the bear was still in the area. I was able to move the people back and work my way around the restrooms and picnic tables to position myself in a good location to take a shot. The bear wandered to within ten yards of me. I carefully aimed the gun toward the bear's rear quarter and pulled the trigger. The dart hit the mark and soon the bear was sleeping soundly.

Since there were so many spectators at this popular picnic spot, I took the opportunity to give a short educational talk to explain what I was doing and why. This was a memorable experience for the visitors and a great opportunity to teach them how to behave in bear country.

I should've called back to the Wildlife Building and asked someone to bring a transfer cage while I gave my little talk, but I didn't. That was the third mistake. I'd darted enough bears by this time to get overly confident. That was my fourth mistake.

When I was ready to take the animal on the five mile drive to the Wildlife Building, I knelt down beside the sleeping bear, slapped my hands, flicked one of its ears, and gently poked its ribs to check if it was fully immobilized. I got no reaction, so I figured the bear was still deeply under the effects of the drugs.

Then I got delayed a few more minutes because people wanted to see the bear up close and take pictures of it. "Can I touch it?" they asked, and because I knew this was a once in a lifetime opportunity for most of them, I said, "Yes, but be sure and wash your hands afterwards."

Bears look beautiful from a distance, but up close they're kind of dirty and they have a smell you'll never forget. It's not pleasant. It's a sour smell, like a person who hasn't taken a bath for six months. But after you've smelled a couple hundred of them, you get used to it.

Bear fur looks thick and shiny from a distance, and the bear usually looks plump, but that's often misleading. You can't really tell what a bear's condition is until you put your hands on it, see the bald spots in its fur, and feel what might be a bag of bones underneath the hair.

When I let people touch the bear, I'd hold the animal's snout with both hands, just in case. Finally I stopped the show because I knew I was cutting it close on how long the drugs would keep the bear asleep. I wasn't really worried though because I thought, *What's a ten minute drive down to the Wildlife Building? What could go wrong during a ten minute drive?*

Famous last words.

I put the unconscious bear behind my seat in the little Jeep, thinking I was home free. I was so wrong. I'll never forget that drive.

It always feels great to drive away from a lot of spectators when things have gone well. As I waved goodbye I was really pumped. My heart was racing and my blood pressure was soaring.

As I drove down the mountain toward the Wildlife Building, I reviewed my performance in front of the crowd and congratulated myself on how well I did, on how much I'd learned in the previous years, and how much I'd improved as a ranger. I was feeling really good about myself. I'd finally made it. I was a professional wildlife biologist!

I kept looking in the rear view mirror to check the traffic behind me because I was on Hwy. 441, the busy two-lane road through the Park. When I neared the Huskey Gap parking area, I crossed a section of road that had been damaged by heavy spring rains. The repair left a big dip in the pavement and when I drove over it, the Jeep bounced hard.

I glanced into the rear view mirror and, instead of seeing the road and cars behind me, all I could see was a bear's eyes and nose. *Ohhh-hhh no!*

That was a real Kodak moment, let me tell you.

I swerved onto to the narrow grassy shoulder of the highway, trying not to jostle the bear, shoved the gearshift into park, left the motor running, and leaped out of the Jeep. I threw my door wide open so the bear would be able to find an easy exit without destroying the vehicle. If the Jeep got torn up I'd have to explain it to my boss and I didn't want to have to do that. The humiliation and the paperwork would be awful.

As I stared at the bear in shock, I became worried that the groggy beast might get out and wander into the highway and be hit by a car. Lots and lots of cars were whizzing by. A hundred horrible possibilities raced through my mind.

One of the most difficult and frustrating aspects of being a wildlife ranger is that every move we make is scrutinized by hundreds of pairs of eyes and second-guessed by countless critics. Our efforts to manage the wild critters in the Park are very transparent to the public. That's both good and bad. Working as a wildlife ranger is fun and rewarding when things go well and we look like heroes, but it's awful when we screw up and the crowd is laughing at us.

I realized I didn't want passersby to notice what was going on, so I tried to act cool, like I had everything under control. That's tough to do when you have a wild bear sitting up in the back of your vehicle.

So far I'd been lucky and the bear remained peaceful. He sat there looking like he was waiting for me to get back in so he could continue his joyride through the Park. I was fairly certain this was the first time this bear had ridden in a Jeep, but he didn't seem to be afraid, probably because of the drugs.

I wasn't nearly as calm as the bear, but I had to do something to try to regain control of the situation. I tried to make as little noise as possible as I moved carefully around the back of the Jeep and opened the door on the passenger side to get my drug kit which was on the front seat.

I prayed the bear wouldn't bite or slap me.

I loaded a jabstick—a pole made like a spear. It had a syringe on one end that would go off when I poked the bear with it. Then I carefully maneuvered the jabstick between the seats and injected the bear in his front shoulder.

The instant I made contact with him, the bear lunged at me and started blowing and popping its jaws. When bears pop their jaws it sounds like a loud version of someone repeatedly smacking their lips.

I'm not sure what he said, but I got the idea that he wasn't my friend at that moment. I'd chased him around the picnic area, shot him with a dart, packed him into the back of a Jeep, and now I was jabbing him with another needle. I'm sure he was ready for me to leave and I would've been happy to oblige, if only I could've.

Thank goodness the bear went back to sleep before he could get out of the Jeep. I hopped back into the driver's seat and raced down to the Wildlife Building without further delay. Fortunately, there were no physical injuries to either me or the bear, and the Jeep was unscathed, but it had certainly been extremely tense for several minutes.

I learned my lesson that time for sure. I promised myself that I'd never *ever* try to drive with a bear in the back seat. If I wasn't going to bother to get a cage, next time I'd at least use a pickup, so the bear couldn't get to me if he happened to wake up unexpectedly.

HUNGRY AS A WOLF

AN ENJOYABLE PART of my job was helping with the reintroduction of an animal species that had been lost to the area for many years. One of the critters we worked with was *Canis rufus*, the red wolf. They're one of the most endangered animals in the world.

Once common, red wolves were nearly wiped out in the early 1900s by predator control programs and loss of habitat. The wolves were already so close to extinction, wildlife specialists had to conduct a captive breeding program of the best specimens they could find before the species was totally lost. They culled out obvious mixes with dogs and coyotes, and were left with fourteen animals.

Captive breeding facilities were established and breeding of this group of animals began. The endangered red wolf population was gradually increased in the carefully protected environment. Next, the U.S. Fish and Wildlife Service looked for areas where red wolves had previously lived that might make good locations to release them into the wild.

At first, they did small releases on islands along the southeastern coast of the U.S., which limited the animals' movements and made them easier to manage. Then, after some success with the wolves on the islands, the Fish and Wildlife Service discussed possibilities for an inland release site.

In 1990 they came to us and asked to release red wolves inside the Great Smoky Mountains National Park. They wanted to see if we could help bring the animals back in the wild. We were happy to try and were cautiously optimistic.

Critters in the Smokies were about to get a new neighbor.

We built acclimation pens in Elkmont, Cades Cove, and Tremont. At first we fed the wolves wild hog carcasses collected from our hog control program and road-killed deer. Wolves can eat a lot of food. Using animal carcasses from the Park was the cheapest and best way to help them get acclimated to prey found in their new home.

The wolf crew kept a close check on the pens and every two or three days we'd throw a portion of a hog carcass over the fence for them. We hoped the wolves would learn to like wild hog meat and help us get rid of the pesky varmints.

Usually, when the first chunk of meat hit the ground the wolves would run over to it, but one day they didn't. We didn't know why they didn't show up. We suspected the wolves were hiding in their dens, which were wooden boxes we'd camouflaged as brush piles. But we couldn't see them, so we weren't sure.

We checked the wolf pen for holes in the fence or tunnels underneath it, but didn't find any breaches in the perimeter. The animals' failure to show up at chowtime was very mysterious. Two days later we came back and threw a quarter of a hog over the fence and, again, no wolves came out. Something was obviously wrong.

This time we went inside the pen to see what was going on. That's when we noticed there were huge bear tracks all over the inside of the pen. We lifted the lid on one of the den boxes and found the wolves inside, cowering.

Apparently a bear had been coming in and stealing the hog carcasses. That surprised us. We hadn't realized that wolves would allow a bear to come in and take their food. Obviously we had a timid wolf pack, or a very bold bear. We were going to have to try to deal with the bear on the wolves' behalf. The wolves were confined and had no chance to hunt for food. They had to be fed by us. But the bear needed to find his own meal in the wild instead of eating what we were providing for the wolves.

To discourage the bear, I decided to try our *capture and release* technique on it.

We didn't want to have to relocate the bear and also we wanted to test our new aversive conditioning strategy. We hoped the experience of being captured would be a negative one that the bear would remember so he'd stay away in the future.

Rick Varner and I carried a bear trap in and placed it near the wolf pen. We caught the bear the very next day. It was a long, lanky bear with a big frame and big feet, but he didn't have much meat on him.

We darted him, examined him, and did a general work up on his condition. Then we gave him the reversal drugs to get him on his merry way.

He was lying about five yards from the edge of the wolf pen. After about ten or fifteen minutes, he started to wake up and get some mobility. I poked him with a stick and shouted at him, trying to scare him away. He wanted to leave, but was still wobbly. I shouted and carried on, poking him in the rear with the stick, following along behind him as he stumbled away.

Each time the bear staggered and fell down, I'd act as terrifying as I could, looming over him, growling, yelling, stomping my feet, slapping trees, and hitting the ground behind him with my stick. I chased him at least a hundred yards up the hollow. I was trying to scare the bear enough that he'd never, *ever*, come back to the wolf pens again.

Well, bears have their limits, just as people do, and this bear had reached his limit with me. As I approached him one more time to go through my rendition of King Kong, the bear decided he'd had enough of me, my stick, and my goofy attempts to act tough. I thought he was still under the effects of the drugs and that he couldn't do anything to me.

I was wrong.

Without any warning, the bear wheeled around at lightning speed and charged me like he'd been shot out of a cannon. Normally you would never want to run from a bear. But this was a different case. I had provoked the bear several times and I'd finally pushed him too far.

Standing my ground in this particular situation wouldn't be the right tactic. I needed to back off, and I did.

Rick said he heard the most horrible crashing noises from tree limbs breaking and looked up to see the rhododendron bushes shaking. Moments later I burst through the brush, running as fast as I possibly could, with the bear right behind me.

Thank goodness the bear was still feeling some effects from the drugs. I was able to win the race back to the wolf pen, but I was only about ten feet ahead of the bear. When he'd chased me back to where we'd started, he was satisfied that I was no longer a threat, and he let me get away. He'd made his point. Fortunately for me, our paths never crossed again.

The next problem we faced with the wolves was that while they were in the acclimation pen, some of them began to get comfortable with the caretaker who came to feed them. This was bad. We didn't want to be teaching the wolves to associate people with food.

We decided to use a technique the U.S. Fish and Wildlife Service had developed. Two or three people would walk in and send the wolf to the back side of the pen. As the wolf ran back and forth along the fence, a person would hold a large fish net in its path and the wolf would run into the net.

Once captured, we'd tie the wolf's legs and secure the animal so it was unable to move. Then the entire wolf crew would stand close around the captured wolf, looming over it. We simply stood over the wolf, reminding it that people were dangerous and that it should run from them.

The Fish and Wildlife Service said this technique for reestablishing human dominance over the wolf was safe for both the animal and the caretakers. It worked. The next day when the caretaker opened the door to feed them, the wolves ran to the far back corner of the pen and stayed there until he left. If I was a wolf, I would've done the same.

After an acclimation period to get the animals used to the sights, sounds, and smells of the Smokies, we opened the gates of the pens and let the wolves come and go as they pleased. We had no idea what to expect, really. The whole project was a genuine experiment.

Most of the wolves stayed in the Park, but a few left. On one occasion, a wolf killed a domestic calf on a farm near the Park boundary in Miller's Cove. Newborn beef calves were easy prey for the wolves and soon this undesirable behavior spread to Cades Cove.

Over a two-week period, the wolves killed nine baby calves that belonged to the Caughron family who'd kept cattle in the cove for many years. The wolves had enough natural instinct in them to know how to hunt in pairs and be successful in bringing down a calf. To survive in the wild, it's important that any predator use the least amount of energy possible to catch its prey. Killing baby domestic beef calves was easy and the wolves thought they were in wolf heaven.

To confirm that the wolves were responsible for killing the baby calves, we sent Rick Varner to the cove to see what was happening. He climbed into a tree stand off Sparks Lane near where some calves had been killed earlier in the week. He watched a newborn baby calf with night vision goggles.

Soon after dark, Rick saw two wolves approach the mother cow and her baby. One of the wolves started fighting with the mother to distract her and lure her away from her defenseless calf. While the battle was going on between the cow and one of the wolves, the other wolf went around and grabbed the baby. The wolves' technique was fast and effective.

After the calves were killed, the Fish and Wildlife Service began to question if the Park was the best place to try to reestablish a population of wolves. They thought about moving to an area without cattle. The wolves hadn't been at the Smokies very long, so we really didn't know if they could survive in the Park or not. To try to help the wolf program continue at least for a little while, we needed to figure out a way to help the mother cows protect their baby calves.

We decided the best option was to build a nursery corral where the cows would have a safe place to give birth and where they could stay until the calves were older. I contacted wildlife fencing experts from Minnesota for advice and they suggested a high-tensile electric fence to keep the wolves and any other predators out. They even agreed to send down their best fence builder to oversee the construction of the fence.

In the hope of keeping the wolf reintroduction going, and to make reparations to the farmer, we fenced off a hundred acres along Sparks Lane. The fence worked and the Fish and Wildlife Service decided not to remove the wolves from the Park.

The fence was effective because anything that touched one of the seven strands of electric wire received over eight thousand volts. That many volts going through your body will sure get your attention. Pushing through the fence wasn't a viable option for wolves, bears, deer, or even a person. I hoped the cows were happy now. The new compound was like a small version of Jurassic Park. I was thankful we didn't need to keep out T-Rex dinosaurs—in comparison, wolves seemed rather easy.

Because the project was experimental, we needed a way to recapture the wolves if something went wrong. We tried putting recapture radio telemetry collars on them. The collar had a GPS unit and two capture darts built into it. This would allow us to locate each animal and capture it remotely without having to use a trap or dart gun.

The darts were loaded with Telazol. It's a relatively safe and effective knockout drug for *canids* like wolves, dogs, and coyotes. The recapture collars also had a detonator that could remotely blow the collar off so you could retrieve it and download information about where the animal had been traveling.

When we first got the collars, they were fairly new on the market and they still had some bugs. We needed to confirm that we could successfully inject immobilization drugs and then find and capture a wild wolf. To test them, we borrowed a dog named Blue. He was a mixed walker-plot hound of a type traditionally used for hunting foxes, bears, or raccoons.

Blue was happy to see us and cooperative about making a visit to the Park. We put one of the new recapture collars on him to test it. Blue and I were stationed in the parking lot just behind Park Headquarters.

Chris Lucash, who headed up the Smokies wolf program for the U.S. Fish and Wildlife Service, had a computer with the software necessary to remotely detonate the dart in Blue's collar. Injecting the drug would be similar to giving the dog a shot at the vet. Chris drove a couple of miles away from Headquarters with his laptop. Once he was in place, he called me on the radio and asked me if I was ready.

I was, and I looked at Blue and he seemed ready, too. So, I gave Chris the green light.

It took Chris three or four minutes to work his way through the recapture software program. During that time Blue was enjoying himself in the parking lot, wagging his tail, running in circles, and rubbing up against me each time he ran by, so I'd pet him.

Then, Chris called and said he was getting ready to activate the collar syringe. I responded with a *10-4*. When Chris hit the button and the dart injected the drug into Blue, the dog's demeanor quickly changed. If you're at the doctor and you know you're getting a shot, I guess you can prepare. But Blue wasn't aware he was about to get a shot, and when it happened, it was definitely a surprise for him.

He ran to me, not understanding what had happened, then ducked between my legs and lay down. He looked up at me in confusion, as if to say, *What was that?* I knelt down and petted him, reassuring him he was okay. He licked my hand and soon forgot about the collar and the shot. A few minutes later he lowered his head, fell sound asleep, and started snoring.

The collar had worked perfectly. Now we were ready to use them on our wolves. As for Blue, we fed him the best meal a dog could ever ask for, then returned him to my friend unharmed. I gave him a big hug, but I don't think he trusted me anymore.

Despite all our efforts, our attempt to reintroduce red wolves ultimately failed. The newborn red wolf pups didn't have the disease resistance they needed to make it. Not a single one of the pups survived.

Because of the wild nature of the adult animals, once they were released into the wilderness, there were limits on the follow-up care we could give them. We could give newborn pups their first shots to protect against distemper, parvo, and other diseases, but then the adults would move the litter and we could rarely find them to provide any additional care.

The prey base of rabbits, quail, and ground hogs was better outside the Park, so some of the wolves left.

A few of the red wolves interbred in the wild with coyotes, which made it nearly impossible to maintain a pure genetic line. Unfortunately, our breeding stock, coming from captivity, didn't have the skill set to survive in the Park setting. By the late 1990s, all of these challenges eventually led the Fish and Wildlife Service to decide to pull their animals out of the Park and move elsewhere.

They captured all the wolves that were wearing radio collars, except for one female running around the Derrick Knob area. She was old and living in a remote area so they decided not to try and capture her. With no male red wolves to breed with, she could've mated with a male coyote, so for a couple of years it's possible there were a few litters of souped-up coyotes living along the Derrick Knob area. But otherwise, the genetically-pure wolves were gone.

Still, even today, people often think they're seeing red wolves in the Park. But they're not. They're seeing coyotes.

The mistake is understandable. The coyotes here in the eastern U.S. are usually bigger than the coyotes in the west. And many of our coyotes have been crossed with feral dogs, which make them less afraid to come in close to people and houses. These dog-coyote hybrids, called *coydogs,* have some traits of a domestic animal in their DNA and in their behavior. They're often larger than normal coyotes and can be seen running through residential areas.

Urban coyotes are becoming more plentiful and they're losing their fear of people.

An adult red wolf is larger than an adult coyote. But it's tough to distinguish between a juvenile red wolf and an adult coyote since they're about the same size. One day I asked Chris Lucash, "How do you guys tell the difference between a young red wolf and a full grown coyote?"

"You look at their neck," Chris said. "If there's radio collar around it, it's a wolf. If not, it's a coyote."

CRYING WOLF

DURING THE TIME THE RED WOLF reintroduction program was in full swing, we were working in Cades Cove darting and capturing whitetail deer as part of a surveillance program for Lyme disease, an infectious tick-borne illness caused by bacteria. We caught nearly fifty deer with the assistance of Dr. John New, a veterinarian from the University of Tennessee.

Dr. New was our go-to vet. He advised us on caring for free-ranging wildlife for many years. He educated us about wildlife diseases, especially the ones that could affect people, like rabies. He also gave us guidance on animal welfare and was our frontline consultant for treatment of sick and injured wild critters.

One January, he was with us in Cades Cove off Sparks Lane when I darted a deer with one of our Pneu-Dart immobilization rifles, which is basically a modified .22 with a barrel large enough to shoot small darts. When we dart a deer, it normally takes five or six minutes for the animal to go down and fall asleep. The drug we use to capture deer is a combination of Telazol and Xylazine. When everything works as it should, the drug knocks the animal out to the point that we could do surgery on it, if we needed to.

This particular adult female deer, when I darted her, ran toward the woods but stopped right at the edge of the field. It was a few minutes before dark and I couldn't see the deer very well from where I was standing. An intern in our group could see her better than I could. I got a radio call. "Hey, Kim," he said, "there are a couple of wolves watching what we're doing."

"Okay," I said. "Keep a close eye on em."

As soon as the drug started taking effect and the deer began to sway and stagger, a young red wolf took off after her at warp speed. "Kim," the intern said, "a wolf's chasing the deer!"

I jumped in my vehicle and tore out slinging gravel in every direction. I raced over to where the deer and wolf had entered the woods. When I got out of my truck, I could hear the deer making a loud distress call, so I took off on foot in the direction of the sound. As I got closer to the screaming deer, I could see that the wolf was riding her down, trying to kill her.

I felt responsible for the deer not being able to run away and didn't want the wolf to take advantage of the situation, so I ran toward it, yelling and screaming at the top of my lungs, "Get outta here wolf!" Then I ended my message with a deep roar, "Grrrrrrrrrr-rrr!"

As I was charging down the hill, waving my arms and growling, the wolf glanced up and saw this overweight Sasquatch-looking creature charging toward him and decided he'd better find another deer. When I got to within twenty yards, the wolf let go and was gone in a flash. Then the deer jumped up and took off down the hollow.

I stood trying to catch my breath and waited for the deer to settle down before walking toward her, because I didn't want her to run any farther away. But before I could get to her, I heard a commotion in the woods below me. I looked toward the sound and could see the wolf running very fast toward the deer. Before I even had time to yell at the wolf it caught up to the deer and jumped on it again!

The deer cried out with a gut-wrenching distress call. Again, I took off yelling, growling, and waving my arms at the wolf. After this second sprint, I not only looked like Sasquatch but sounded like him, too.

The wolf wanted nothing to do with me. When he turned around and saw me running toward him, he jumped up and took off. He'd have to have to go to bed hungry that night.

This time I caught up with the deer before she could get up. I gently lay on the deer giving it and me some time to catch our breath, cool off, and calm down. The deer might not have known it, but she was in safe hands now. All I wanted to do was get her weight and collect a hair and blood sample. Then she'd be free to go back and join the other deer.

I held her down and gave her another half-dose of immobilization drugs, which can be a little tricky when an animal is trying its best to get up. After the drugs kicked in, the deer finally went to sleep, and I was able to collect what we needed for our research.

Then I gave her the reversal drug, and after a few minutes, she woke up, jumped up, and took off. She ran about forty yards away, then stopped and looked back at me. I don't know if she was thanking me or hoping that a big truck would run over me!

The wolf had leaped on top of the galloping deer twice, and held on with its mouth, but because the wolf was primarily concerned with trying to hang on, it hadn't had time to do any serious damage. I'm sure the deer had quite a story to tell the other deer when she got home, though.

I suspected that afterwards, if she ever saw a white Explorer driving toward her with a big guy hanging out the window holding a dart gun, she'd run for the hills.

I wouldn't blame her.

BEAR BREAKOUT

IT WAS LATE JULY when a mother bear and her two cubs were reported to be terrorizing Cosby Campground trying to get food from unsuspecting campers. Raising cubs can put a strain on a mother bear. A shortage of natural food can also contribute to a family group looking for human food in a campground. But regardless of the reason, a situation like this couldn't be allowed to continue.

As soon as we got the report, I loaded up my equipment and drove to Cosby. It wasn't hard to find the bear family. All I had to do was look for the big crowd of people. I was lucky and the capture went smoothly. In no time I had all three bears loaded into a transfer cage and was on my way back to Park Headquarters.

We moved the mother and her cubs into a ten-by-fourteen-by-six-foot chain link holding cage in the Wildlife Building. I'd had the pen built years earlier to hold a bear that bit a lady in Elkmont. The lady's husband, who was a doctor, wanted us to hold the bear for a while and monitor it for any signs of rabies. The bear turned out to be healthy, so we were able to release it at the end of the observation period. We kept the cage and it frequently came in handy.

The mother bear and her two cubs were settled down in the holding pen where they'd stay until we could find a good place to release them. Our plan was to move the family group the next day. This sounded relatively simple and straightforward, but we were working with wild animals. That meant things didn't always go as planned.

This was one of those times.

The next morning when we got to work and went in to check on the family group, we were shocked at what we found. The two cubs were in the holding cage, but the mother bear wasn't. She was gone.

Somehow she'd managed to get out during the night. When we inspected the cage, we saw where she'd escaped. She'd pulled on the chain-link with her teeth and claws until she'd spread the wire far enough apart to create a hole she could squeeze through.

We've learned the hard way that if a bear can get its head through a hole, usually its body will be able to squeeze through behind it, and the bear can get out. This mother bear was able to distort the wire enough to get free. Then she pushed a glass window open and escaped from the Wildlife Building.

We wondered if she'd deserted her two cubs or if she was hiding nearby in the woods, waiting for them to follow her. This wasn't a good situation. I was responsible for those cubs and I really didn't know what I should do next.

Contrary to what many people might think, mother bears won't always fight to the death for their cubs, especially young mother bears. I'm not saying that *all* mother bears won't fight for their cubs. I'm just saying that some will and some won't. In some cases, where the defense of her cubs means the mother is jeopardizing her own life, she may not be as protective as in other situations. I suppose it's a survival instinct.

Also, just like with people, there are good mother bears and not-so-good mother bears. In any case, it's best to never approach *any* bear—with or without cubs. You could be jeopardizing your life.

When we realized the mother bear had left the area and abandoned her two cubs, our hearts sank. What were we supposed to do with two orphaned cubs? They were too young to release. They'd never be able to make it on their own. And because it was summer, no mother bears were sleeping in dens, so we had no chance to place the cubs with an adoptive mother. Appalachian Bear Rescue didn't exist yet.

We were in a bind, so we started brainstorming. We decided our first and best option was to put the two cubs in a medium-sized cage and set them just outside the fence that ran around the Wildlife

Building and maintenance compound. Then we'd put a large culvert-style trap next to it. I was fairly confident the mother bear would come back during the night to get her cubs.

We did this for two nights in a row, but, as far as we could tell, the mother bear never came back. I was feeling guilty for catching the family group, especially now that the cubs might be orphaned forever. I needed all the help I could get, so I prayed hard for divine intervention.

I tried to think of other options. I remembered the days when we captured and released nuisance bears in the Park. In most cases, the nuisance bears tended to go right back to where we'd captured them, because the location was usually within their home territory. I wondered if this mother bear might do the same and return to Cosby Campground.

I called out to Cosby and explained to the rangers what had happened and asked them to please let me know immediately if they had any bears show up out there. Most bears have *extremely* strong homing instinct. Since the mother bear wasn't in the area she escaped from, I prayed she'd go back home to Cosby.

Cosby Campground was about thirty miles away from the Wildlife Building as the crow flies. That's a long, long way on foot, especially traveling up and down the steep mountains through brush and briars and thickets. But bears are amazing and intelligent creatures so traveling thirty miles in a few days wouldn't be unheard of.

Sure enough, the next day I got the call I was praying for. A tagged, adult, female bear had showed up in Cosby Campground and was active in the area where I'd caught the family group three days earlier. I was excited and hopeful it was the bear we were looking for. There was a chance now that this story could have a happy ending.

I threw my gear into my truck and immediately went out there to try to catch her again. On my way to Cosby, I might've exceeded the speed limit a little bit. When I arrived, I saw the bear. I darted her and as soon as she was asleep, I approached her to look at her ear tags. *Thank you Lord*, I thought. It was the mother bear. I took her back to the Wildlife Building again with a big smile on my face.

When I got there, I put her into the newly-repaired cage with her cubs and they started nursing immediately. What a beautiful sight. Now that we had them back together again, we were able to relocate the family to a more remote area outside the Park. We decided to release them in a bear sanctuary in the Cherokee National Forest where we hoped they'd be less tempted by human food and could live in a relatively safe location.

When we got them to their new home and opened the door of the transfer cage, the mother bear and her two cubs jumped out and ran up an old logging road. Before they were out of sight, though, one of the cubs stopped and turned around to look at us. I'm not sure what it was thinking, but I guess it might've been, *Thanks for bringing Mom back.*

The family quickly disappeared into the thick brush. We got no reports of problems with them in their new home. So that made all the hard work worthwhile.

NO GOOD DEED GOES UNPUNISHED

WILDLIFE RANGERS are very concerned about the animals in the Park. We dedicate our lives to working with them. We worry about the health of all wild animals, but especially those that are fed human food. Some people do this just so an animal will come in closer for a photo. These people aren't very considerate about protecting the animals. They're only thinking of themselves and not about the wildlife.

One important downside in feeding critters human food is that it's very bad for the animals' teeth. Good teeth are essential for their survival. Bears that eat garbage can get tooth problems, and there's no dentist in the wild who can help them, so they suffer. In some cases, their suffering can go on for a long time. Bad teeth can be a major factor in causing an animal's death.

Even more worrisome is that the irresponsible, unconcerned people who teach wild animals to associate food with humans cause the creature to be potentially dangerous to the next person they encounter.

We do everything in our power to prevent this, but we're vastly outnumbered. There are nine million tourists who visit the Park every year, but only a handful of us who are assigned exclusively to manage wildlife. The entire wildlife department is three full-time and three part-time employees.

That's six people total, to handle most of the wildlife issues in 800 square miles. And three of them are just part-time! Of course other Park staff, and even visitors, lend a helping hand to protect our animals, but still, we've had to learn to do the best we can with what we have.

Some people are very naïve about biology and wild animals. They've spent most of their life on concrete or sitting in a comfortable office chair, and they've forgotten that nature can be harsh and cruel.

One example of this dangerously poor judgment happened when a couple from Florida who were driving around the Cades Cove Loop and saw a yearling bear trying to kill a deer fawn for food. They decided to intervene to save the fawn's life. Common sense should tell you that it's extremely dangerous to get between a bear, or any predator, and its intended prey.

It's also illegal to intervene in natural feeding habits of the animals in the Park, no matter how sad it is to see the reality of life in the wild.

The Florida couple ran through the field and attacked the young bear. Visitors who saw the incident said the man kicked the bear until he finally got it off the fawn. Then he grabbed the small bear with his bare hands and threw it in up the air, and continued to kick and chase it across the field until it ran out of sight.

Once the bear was chased away, the couple went back to their car and continued their trip around the Loop road. Visitors reported the situation to rangers at Cades Cove Visitor Center, and rangers were able to stop the couple as they left the cove and give both of them tickets for harassing wildlife.

Things could've gone very bad when the man grabbed the wild bear. Even a small bear has fearsome teeth and claws that can seriously injure a person or even kill them. That man was luckier than he realized. This was one of those situations where I wondered, *What were they thinking?*

Our wildlife program has always been open to public view. We're used to having people watch how we do our jobs. Although most visitors are supportive of how we manage the Park's wildlife, some of them are critical of our decisions. That's not always bad, but with some people, we'll never win. It's especially unpleasant when we're criticized on the basis of insufficient or wrong information. All we can do then is perform our jobs the best we can, and move on.

An example of being criticized over misinformation happened when we got a report of a mother bear with three cubs causing some serious problems at Spence Field Shelter. It was in the spring, which is a little early for bears to be active at backcountry campsites. We try to educate backpackers about food and garbage, and we work to keep the site as clean as possible, but keeping bears and people separated in the backcountry is virtually impossible.

Although we did our best to keep the bear family away from Spence Field Shelter, we weren't successful. We'd used just about everything in our bear management toolbox on both the backpackers and this family of bears. But the bears knew how to outsmart campers to get their food and a few of the backpackers did very little to prevent it. We got reports that some people intentionally fed the bear from inside the protection of the chain link front wall of the shelter.

We decided that rounding up the bear family and moving them to a remote area outside the Park would probably be the best strategy to protect the campers and give the animals a chance to continue living in the wild. If we left the bears where they were, they could become more aggressive in getting food from campers and eventually someone might get hurt.

Another reason we needed to move the bears as soon as possible was that neither the Tennessee Wildlife Management Agency nor the U.S. Forest Service would accept an aggressive bear for relocation. I'd never offer them an animal that was a threat to people, either. So, relocating them now was our last option before being forced to euthanize the entire family. I didn't want to have to do that.

I made arrangements to have a helicopter on call to come pick up the mother bear and her three cubs when I had them ready. I needed a helicopter because carrying the bears out of the backcountry would require keeping the animals immobilized with drugs for a long time and we knew from experience that they could die from this. It was a risk I wasn't willing to take. Using a helicopter would cost a bunch more money, but it would be worth it.

So, I gathered my drugs and my dart pistol, and went to catch the bear and her cubs. I didn't have long to wait until the mother bear wandered up the Eagle Creek Trail to the shelter looking for a handout. Her cubs followed right behind her in single file.

I estimated her weight at 140 pounds, so I prepared a dart with 3 cc's of a Rompum/Ketamine mixture. When she positioned herself so I had a good angle, I shot my C02 powered dart pistol. The dart hit its mark, made its normal pop, and in five minutes she went to sleep next to the Spence Field Shelter.

When you're trying to work with a mother and cubs, you always dart the mother first. You do it that way because if you do anything that looks aggressive to a cub in front of its mother, you can get one very angry mother bear after you. But because the cubs will stay near their mother in most any situation, you can dart her first, and they'll usually be easy to catch once she's asleep.

Usually, but not always.

In this case, after the mother went to sleep, one of the cubs stayed next to her, but the other two climbed a tree. They didn't climb very high, so I loaded a dart pistol with a very small dart of Ketamine only, because it's not safe to give other drugs like Rompun to cubs.

Rompun suppresses their breathing too much and causes their little bodies to heat up like an oven. This fatally overheated condition, called *hyperpyrexia*, is a side effect of the tranquilizer we use. And the malignant, feverish reaction to the drugs can easily cause death.

Using Ketamine by itself makes a cub's muscles a bit stiff—they move like they're in slow motion—so it's easy to handle them. And the drug wears off quickly, so it's much safer for them.

The two tree-climbing cubs were obviously unhappy that mom wasn't there to help them. As I approached the tree, both cubs extended their upper lips and started blowing at me, which is a defensive move on their part to let me know I wasn't welcome. I pointed the pistol at the cub's hip and gently pulled the trigger. Then I did the same for the second cub. Fortunately the darts found their marks and both cubs were soon groggy and fell out of the tree into my arms. I put them into a little transfer cage until I could catch their sibling.

Capturing the third cub, though, was a different story. I'd classify him as a *ground runner.* Whenever I approached him, he took off. Most cubs, when they get scared, go up a tree and wait for orders from mom, but a very small percentage of them will go horizontal and run like a jackrabbit. This time I had a ground runner and these cubs are nearly impossible to catch by darting them, because I couldn't get close enough for a shot.

I chased that little rascal all over Spence Field and around the spring which was a hundred yards behind the shelter, but I could neither catch it nor dart it. This was a serious problem. It's precisely what you *don't* want to happen. Over and over the cub would let me get to within about fifteen yards of him and then he'd take off. He'd get away and then stop and look at me as if to say, *I'm too fast for you.*

He was right.

I didn't want to separate any of the cubs from their momma, but I couldn't leave the mother bear immobilized for very long, either. I needed to call the helicopter and get her down to Cades Cove for transport to the Wildlife Building. I wasn't sure what to do. I wondered if I should abort the whole mission. I called my boss, Bill

Cook, and described the situation.

He said to take the mother and the two cubs I had, and leave the other cub for the time being. I didn't like leaving a cub behind, but it was a sensible compromise. I was relieved I didn't have to make the decision myself, because I knew being left behind could spell doom for the third cub.

I didn't want the little cub to die, so, after I called the helicopter to come to Spence Field, I quickly set up a Havahart trap, a small humane live trap, just above the Spence Field spring and baited it with marshmallows.

When the helicopter came, we laid the mother, who was still sleeping soundly, in the floor in the back. Then we loaded the two cubs I'd caught, both of which were now fully awake, into the back seat of the helicopter. As we lifted off the ground, I looked down toward where the remaining cub was hiding. I'm sure he was scared out of his mind and hoping to be reunited with his family, but he was all alone now.

We made a quick flight down to Cades Cove, loaded the bears into a transfer cage, and hauled them to the Wildlife Building to hold until we captured the remaining cub. I knew the little guy would be running around looking for his momma and wondering where everyone was. We'd do our best to get him reunited with his family as soon as possible. I knew he was facing a long night with little sleep and I'm sure he was very hungry.

When cubs are separated from their mother, most will cry for help until mom returns. But mom wasn't coming to his rescue this time. He was on his own. If he'd climbed up a tree for me, we'd be in good shape, but he didn't. Although my boss had made the decision to separate the family, I still felt responsible. I had a sick feeling in my stomach.

My intention was to return to Spence Field early the next morning. But late that evening I was asked to hike to Derrick Knob the following morning to check out some smoke from a possible fire. At the time, manpower was limited because the Park had several active fires and crews were out working on them. Now I needed to find someone else to hike to Spence Field and check on the trap.

Before I went to bed that night I called one of our summer interns, Robert, to hike up to Spence very early the next morning, in the dark, before daybreak. I told him the whole story and stressed that he had to be there by daylight in order to prevent hikers from finding and possibly releasing the cub. But my biggest concern was the threat from a possible predator.

If a cub was in the trap, it was an easy target and could be killed by other animals, the biggest threat being territorial male bears. I knew dominant male bears would kill cubs to protect their territory. I was seriously worried for the little cub's safety.

Robert was excited about the opportunity to save the cub. He got up bright and early the next morning and charged up the mountain on the five mile hike to Spence Field. As he approached the shelter at daybreak, he could hear the cub screaming bloody murder. He sprinted down the trail toward the spring, thinking something was killing the little bear.

When he got close enough to see the Havahart trap, he could tell there was a small black fur ball in the cage. Wonderful! He had him. But before he started celebrating, he saw some movement in the weeds above the trapped cub. As he approached, he saw a huge male bear sitting on a big rock looking intently at the cub. Robert started throwing rocks and yelling, "Get outta here bear!"

He screamed repeatedly and acted aggressive toward the big bear until he managed to chase the beast away. It was a close call for the cub. In a few more minutes it might've been a goner and this story would've had a very sad ending.

Robert tied the trap, with the cub still in it, inside his backpack where the cub would ride better, and it would be easier to carry. If he carried the cage in his hand, the cub would keep snapping and slashing at him through the wire and also he'd have to stop and explain to everybody who saw him why he was carrying a cub around in a trap.

He carried the little feller down the mountain and soon we reunited it with its family. They were all happy to see each other again. I don't know if bears smile but, if they do, that little guy was smiling.

After the Tennessee Wildlife Resources Agency and the U. S. Forest Service gave the okay to release the family group on their property, we took the bear family to the Ocoee Bear Sanctuary on the border between Tennessee and Georgia. In this remote area they'd have the best chance of living their lives free and wild.

The public is very concerned about how we do our jobs. People are interested in the welfare of each and every animal in the Park. For that reason, our treatment of animals provokes a lot of comment. Many of the comments are intelligent, but some of them aren't. We try to deal with everyone as diplomatically as possible.

At the time of these events, there were a few people who were very vocal about wanting the Park Service to have a *hands off* approach toward all the animals in the Park. They wanted us to leave the bears totally alone, to not manage the Park wildlife in any way.

An activist, Eddie Jefferson, heard something about what was happening. He hiked up to Spence Field and was giving out informational leaflets at the junction of the Bote Mountain and Appalachian Trail after I'd flown the mother and two cubs out of the backcountry. He was totally unaware that we'd set a trap at the spring for the third cub and planned to hike back up there the next morning to get him. He was telling people that I'd deserted a baby cub and left it to starve.

I had a two-inch thick file full of Congressional inquiries, letters, and allegations made by this one fellow. Eddie was always critical of some aspect of our wildlife management programs. He forced me to spend a lot of time answering Congressional inquiries and responding to his allegations. The time I spent dealing with him was time taken away from helping animals.

Eddie spent a lot of time in Cades Cove doing wildlife photography, some of which turned out to be commercial. He often got very close to deer and bears to photograph them. He wanted other people kept away, but he didn't mind closing the distance himself. He came across as a person who wanted to protect wildlife, but it seemed to me that his own personal financial gain might've been a factor.

Over my career, I'd say we received 99.9% support for the way we managed the Park's wildlife. But there will always be a very small percentage of people who you just can't please. Democracy is good, but sometimes it's not particularly informed. This can make a ranger's job an even bigger challenge. It's tough enough to manage wildlife, but when you add people management into the mix, it can be impossible at times.

RANGER AND SON

WHEN HE WAS TEN YEARS OLD, I took my son, Travis, to work with me, to show him what I did on the job. I hoped he'd be interested in following in my footsteps as a wildlife biologist.

My first task for the day was to capture a mother bear and her two cubs and move them away from the Chimneys picnic area where they were causing problems and foraging through garbage.

Since I was going to be using immobilization drugs, I made a radio request for assistance from any Park employees who might be in the area. Jerry Grubb came to help me. Jerry was a law enforcement ranger who worked in the North District. He was a very tough and very brave guy. I always thought of him as the sheriff in *Walking Tall*. If I was ever in need of help from a ranger when my life was in jeopardy from another human, my first choice would be Jerry.

When I arrived at the picnic area, the cries and screams of visitors quickly indicated the location of the bear and her two cubs. The mother looked to be about 150 pounds, so normally I'd give her about three cc's of our immobilization cocktail.

But because we were so close to the parking lot, I decided to give her two cc's. That would give us enough time to get the mother bear down the short nature trail and into the transfer cage. I was also concerned that if I kept her asleep too long while her cubs were awake, they might damage her eyes as they crawled around on her. So I gave her a lighter dose than normal.

I stalked the mother bear and got close enough for an easy fifteen-yard shot. The dart hit its mark and within four minutes she started to look groggy. Then she lay down and was soon asleep. Once the mother was immobilized, the two cubs ran up a tree.

While the cubs hid in a tree, I loaded a pistol with a small 1 cc dart. I darted the cub in its rear leg and soon the first little bear fell out of the tree and into our catch net. We easily captured the second cub as well. I laid the cubs alongside their sleeping momma on a wheeled stretcher of the same type we used to haul injured people out of the backcountry. That way we could carry the entire bear family to the truck in one load.

Jerry and my son Travis were going to help me carry the stretcher down the trail and load the family into a transport cage in the back of the *Boar*, a half-ton Dodge four-wheel drive pickup truck. My two helpers had the head end of the stretcher and I was at back.

I should've known better than to put them on the front of the stretcher, where the mother bear's head would be close to their hands, just in case anything happened, but it was a short trip to the truck, so I didn't think much about it.

When we got on a steep, rough part of the trail, we were stumbling along trying to avoid exposed rocks and roots. The stretcher was jerking and jiggling quite a bit. Because I was taller and uphill from them, I was having trouble holding my end of the stretcher level with their end. I remember Travis saying, "Dad, shouldn't we strap her in?"

"No, son," I said. "We've only got a little way to go. We'll be back at the truck in a jiffy."

Our staggering downhill was causing the unconscious mother bear to slide toward Jerry and Travis. Travis's face was on the same level as the mother bear's head. I didn't realize it at the time, but years later Travis told me the mother bear's front teeth were continually rubbing against the hand he was using to carry the litter, but he was trying to be brave and didn't say anything about it.

When we were within sight of my truck, the jouncing of the litter roused the bear just a little bit and she opened her eyes and raised her head to look up at us. That wasn't good. Then she suddenly raised up on her front legs. This put her in a position where she was looking

Jerry right in the eye and she was looming over Travis' head.

Jerry and Travis instantly dropped their end of the stretcher and ran off down the trail. All I could see of them as they retreated was heels and elbows. Apparently it was every man for himself.

When they let go of their end of the stretcher, it turned over in the trail and the family of bears rolled off onto the ground. This stimulated the mother bear even more and she tried to stand up.

I jumped to the front end of the stretcher and grabbed the mother bear. I held her head down with one hand while I struggled to prepare a syringe with the other. Obviously I needed to give her another injection as quickly as possible. I wished I'd given her the normal amount of drugs in the first place but, as they say, hindsight is 20-20.

I was in a rush, let me tell you. And it didn't help that I was having to work mostly one-handed because I had to keep the mother bear's head under control. I held the syringe in my mouth as I took the bottle of immobilization drugs out of the tackle box. I was highly motivated, so even one-handed, I was able to work pretty fast. I was also very fortunate and the bear didn't revive enough to bite or scratch me, or run away.

When I finally got more drugs into her and she fell back asleep, I looked down at the vehicles and saw two heads peeking around the side of Jerry's patrol cruiser. I hollered down to them, "Are you guys okay?"

It took a *lot* of reassurance that the bear was asleep, but I was finally able to convince Jerry and Travis to come back up the trail and help me. When they'd satisfied themselves that the bear was definitely unconscious, they helped me reload the family onto the stretcher and carry them the rest of the way to my truck.

We were lucky there wasn't a big crowd standing around to watch and critique our performance. None of us would've gotten a very good score I'm afraid, but the audience would certainly have had a good laugh.

This wasn't the kind of situation I'd intended to get my little boy into. As you might guess, Travis didn't choose wildlife management as a career. He points to this incident as the main reason.

THE BIOLOGIST AND THE THREE BEARS

SOMETIMES YOUNG CUBS will leave a ground den for a little exploring before their momma is ready to wake up. In one case where a family had denned on a steep bank in Crib Gap beside Laurel Creek Road near the entrance to Cades Cove, a cub crawled out of the den while its mom was still snoozing and accidently rolled down the bank and landed next to the highway.

One of our wildlife crew, Dan Nolfi, retrieved the cub and carried it up the bank and returned it to the ground den where its mother lay. Within a day or so the cub rolled back down the hill and was found beside the road a second time. Again, Dan carried the cub back up the steep bank to the den, but this time he built a fence of natural debris around the den to prevent the cub from taking another tumble down the bank.

Several days later, Dan checked the den and the family of bears was gone.

Our bears rarely use the same den from year to year. And it's not uncommon for bears, including mother bears with newborn cubs, to change the locations where they den during the winter.

We'd already had a couple of cases in the Park that year where cubs had been found without a mother in the area. In one situation, a lone cub had been found along a hiking trail, and in the other, two cubs had wandered up to the side of Newfound Gap Road near the Huskey Gap parking area. It would be extremely unusual, however, for someone walking around in the woods to come across *three* baby bears without their mother.

The rangers confiscated the three newborn cubs from a guy who said he found them lying on the ground when he was hiking off-trail in the Panther Creek area between Chilhowee Lake and Parson

Branch Road. We found this story suspicious.

We now had three two-pound cubs on our hands. What were we supposed to do with them? There aren't a lot of options with orphan cubs. In the early years, we had very little experience placing orphans with adoptive mothers, so we weren't really sure how to go about it. Then we heard about Gary Alt, a well-known bear researcher in Pennsylvania, who'd successfully placed cubs with adoptive mothers. We decided to give it a try.

It was cold, in the dead of winter. We needed to find a mother with a cub of her own already in the den with her. We went to a place where the University of Tennessee bear researchers knew there was a mother bear hibernating in a ground den on a sloped bank located in the Flats between the Sugarlands Visitor Center and the entrance to Elkmont.

We decided to see if we could get the mother bear to adopt these three little orphan cubs. We weren't sure if our plan would work, but we didn't know what else to do. The Appalachian Bear Rescue Center didn't exist yet, so our options were extremely limited.

Bill Stiver, a University of Tennessee bear researcher at the time, went along with the group for our first try at bear adoption in the wild. The researchers used radio telemetry to show us exactly where to take the orphaned cubs.

We were a bit concerned about visiting the den in the first place. As you get closer to the time bears naturally emerge from their dens in the spring, any disturbance can cause them to wake up and run away. If this happened, the mother might desert her own cub. That would be a disaster. Then we'd have four cubs without a mother.

We climbed up the bank, found the den, and peeked in. I shined a flashlight in and could see a bear curled up in a small hole she'd dug into the bank. It was a tense situation. We were whispering and using hand signals to communicate. I positioned myself so I could roll out of the way if the mother bear decided to bolt out of the den.

The mother bear slowly raised her head and looked at us. I motioned for someone to give me the first cub. We didn't dare reach into the den with our hands, so we sent the first cub in using a catchpole, a round aluminum pipe with a cable loop on one end. I put the cable loop around the little cub. Then, while my boss, Bill Cook, held the flashlight, I slowly eased the cub closer and closer to the mother bear.

When the little feller got close enough, the mother bear stretched her neck and sniffed at it. This was do or die time. If she tried to bite the strange cub, I hoped I could jerk it back out quickly enough to save it. If she accepted the new addition to her family, I'd move the cub in closer.

I wondered what the cub was thinking when it looked at the large unfamiliar bear in the den. I guessed it was something like, *That's not my Momma! I hope she likes me.* The cub was within a foot of the mother bear.

The big bear slowly rose up on her front legs. Before I could do anything, she extended her paw and pulled the cub close like a gambler raking in chips at a Las Vegas gaming table. She swept the cub all the way in next to her own cub to accept it, feed it, care for it, and keep it warm.

We repeated the process for the two other cubs and each time, the mother bear pulled the baby in and accepted it. I looked in one last time and the new cubs were pushing and rooting their way closer to the protection of their new mom. Before I turned to slide down the bank, I could hear the distinctive purring noise of the cubs nursing. It's a loud sound similar to someone typing fast on an old-style typewriter.

We were all *so* relieved. I knew we'd given three little orphans another chance to continue to live in the wild. Even though I was wet, dirty, and freezing, this was the kind of day that really made me love my job.

A SCHOOL FOR BEARS

I'VE MADE SO MANY MISTAKES over the years in the process of learning how to handle bears. I'm sure there are lots of embarrassing and scary goofs I can't even remember, and it's a relief that I don't. But one I'll *never* forget was when I made the decision to go to the Wildlife Building and do a workup on a nuisance bear by myself.

It was on a Sunday afternoon and calling someone in to work would've required overtime. Conducting a biological workup on a sedated black bear really requires the help of two people. But my conservative nature was to spend as little money as possible and doing it alone would be cheaper. Cheaper, but not smarter.

Not calling anyone in to help was my first mistake.

Bears have a hard time regulating their temperature when they're drugged. So during the summer months we normally perform bear work-ups in an air-conditioned room. I took the bear to the office in the Wildlife Building. That seemed like a good idea at the time. After all, the bear was asleep. I thought nothing could happen. At this point, I'd done over a hundred bear workups. I was a professional. At least that's what I kept telling myself. *What could go wrong?*

My inflated sense of confidence was my second mistake.

I performed the usual procedures we did on a bear that had been coming too close to people or to garbage. I pulled a nonfunctional tooth, the first premolar, then I put a numbered tag in the bear's ear, recorded a series of measurements, collected a blood sample, looked for ticks and other parasites, and all the other things we normally did to assess a bear's overall condition.

I did this because I knew that the biological work-up was an experience the bear needed. If it was performed at the right time, on night-active bears caught in picnic areas or campgrounds, this procedure provided the bear with an unhappy experience of being around humans. It worked extremely well to discourage bears that were just starting to experiment with coming around people.

I wasn't in a rush because I knew this type of *aversive conditioning* was the most effective and humane way to try and save the bear's life. It was like a reform school for bears. In simple terms, we were trying to create a negative experience associated with people that was more memorable than any positive experiences they'd had around humans like, for example, getting their food.

In the Smokies, humans are pretty much the only predators that black bears need to worry about. In the wild, they're much safer from cars and poachers and junk food, and they live a longer and healthier life. People can really mess things up for wild animals.

I finished working on the bear in the air-conditioned office and was making a call to Jack Piepenbring, the Cades Cove District Ranger, to discuss where we might try to relocate the animal. I was thinking of releasing it at the end of Parson Branch Road and this area was under Jack's supervision. Apparently I got a little long-winded on the telephone and wasn't paying as much attention to the bear's level of sedation as I should've been.

That was my third mistake.

I was relaxed and thought I had things under control. I had my ankles crossed and boots propped up on the desk. My arms were behind my head and I was stretched out like I was in my easy chair at home. The 250-pound bear was lying on a stainless steel work table about three feet from my toes.

At some point in the conversation I picked up the ear tagging tool and was playing with it. Then I accidentally dropped it onto the desk. It made a loud clanging noise. I saw the bear's ear twitch at the sound, and his head move slightly. That was a signal for me to hang up.

I thought to myself, *This is not good.* I knew I should've been keeping a better check on the bear's level of sedation. If a bear is able to twitch its ears or even slightly move its head or legs, get ready, because the animal is gonna wake up soon. I was about to relearn this lesson the hard way.

"Jack," I said, "I think this bear's wakin up and I'm gonna have to go."

Then I hung up the phone. The clatter of the receiver going back down into the cradle was just enough additional stimulation to rouse the bear. He raised his head and looked at me at eye level. Then he stood straight up on the table and towered over me.

I froze. The bear and I stared at each other for what seemed like three days, but probably wasn't more than fifteen seconds. I asked myself, *What was I thinking?*

Obviously I hadn't been thinking much. But this was the last thing I expected to happen. Now I was trapped in the far corner of a concrete block room—away from the door—with no possible exit unless the bear moved out of the way.

I looked around, trying to decide what to do, but there was nothing I *could* do. I was cornered by the bear. Although he was groggy, he was fully capable of doing serious damage to me.

The bear was standing up, swaying like a drunk as he looked at me. Then he lunged and fell off the table. He landed on the floor between me and my drug kit. So, I was still trapped.

Thank goodness I'd left the office door partially open, so when the bear scrambled up from the floor, he noticed the open door and stumbled out, trying to find the woods. I grabbed my drug kit and ran after him.

The bear was so groggy, he didn't go very far. He lumbered away, and then paused near the gas pumps where Park employees fuel their government vehicles. That gave me time to load a dart and sneak up behind him close enough to shoot him again.

After he was darted, he walked only a few feet before lying down and going back to sleep beside the gas pumps. I was extremely happy that no rangers or Park employees needed gas at that moment. If they had, they would've gotten more octane than they were looking for.

I ran down to the Wildlife Building and returned as fast as I could, rolling a gurney. I was able to grab the bear around his chest and load him onto the gurney and take him back inside. I was extremely grateful that no one had seen my stupid mistake.

The next day we relocated the bear inside the Park and he did fine in his new home.

I've had several flashbacks involving a big bear standing up on a table, looming over me, trying to decide what he wanted to do with me. The bear's instinctive intimidation strategy had worked extremely well. For a while, he was completely in charge. But thanks to the Good Lord watching out for me, there was a happy ending for both of us.

LET ME OUTTA HERE!

AFTER SEVERAL YEARS of working in the Park, I got more experience with wildlife than I could ever have imagined. That was good, because the wild hog problem was getting worse.

As part of a government natural resource protection program, we were given about $300,000 a year for three years as part of an intensive effort to reduce their population. This extra money meant I was able to hire several younger wildlife handlers, technicians, and interns to help.

Now I'd be directing a small army of hog hunters and trappers who'd have to go through as steep a learning curve as I had. Supervising new people would be great, I thought, because now maybe some of the goofs wouldn't be my fault!

One of the very best of the wildlife technicians I ever hired was Rick Varner. Rick is like a cross between MacGyver and Rambo. He's a former Marine who is well trained in survival skills and firearms. He can design, fix, or improve just about anything. He can climb mountains like he's walking on flat ground. He's an extremely hard worker and a dang good one. He sets the standard for others to aim for.

An intern named Craig Johnson was assigned to help Rick part-time during the summer. Craig had never seen a bear and he was very nervous about them. His first encounter didn't go well, either. Rick came by to tell me about it.

"You know the injured momma bear and her three cubs we captured?" Rick said.

I nodded.

"The mother bear was taken down to the vet school for treatment and while she was in the hospital, I kept her three cubs in our holding facility at the Wildlife Building.

"When the momma bear had recuperated and it was time to release her, we decided to return her to Cades Cove. That meant I needed to take the cubs to the cove so we could release the whole family together. I asked Craig to help me.

"The cubs weighed about twenty-five pounds apiece. Because they were so little, I didn't want to have to use any drugs on em."

Rick and I both understood that a twenty-five-pound bear cub wasn't harmless. It was like dealing with a cross between a raccoon and a bobcat on a heavy regimen of steroids.

"My plan was to just grab the cubs," Rick said, "and put em into the transfer cage without darting em or using any tranquilizers."

Cubs have an even tougher time regulating their body temperatures when they're immobilized than adult bears do. So, to keep them from becoming overheated and possibly dying, we prefer to use only physical restraint on them, which means the chances of getting bitten and scratched are extremely high. But that's just part of the job.

"The cubs were in the medium-sized holding pen," Rick said. "When Craig and I approached em, they ran to the opposite side of the pen and climbed up the side of the chain link to about five feet high and clung there.

"I told Craig the plan was that we'd just wade in there and grab one cub at a time and hand-carry em to the transfer cage. I warned him that when you grab a cub that size by the scruff of the neck, they'd claw your arm, but it wouldn't hurt too bad.

"'What do you mean *too bad?*' he said. Then he suggested, 'You do the first one and I'll watch. Then I'll do the next one.'

"I said, 'It's a deal.'

"I had him open the door to the pen and I stooped down and

went inside. I plucked one of the cubs off the side of the cage where it was clinging, Craig opened the door for me, and I backed out of the pen, and put the cub into the transfer cage.

"'Okay, now it's your turn,' I said.

"'No,' he said, 'I think I'd better watch you do another one. I'll get the last one.'

"I agreed, and went inside the cage. The remaining cubs ran up the chain link again, so I pulled one of em off the wire, and transferred it to the new cage.

"Then I said, 'Okay, this last one's yours.'

"Craig went inside the pen and the remaining cub retreated, but this time it didn't climb the chain link. This cub stayed on the floor. And when Craig approached it, the cub ran through his legs."

Rick didn't have to say it. We both knew that bears were smart. They learned things. That cub wouldn't climb the cage wall because it saw what happened to the other two. Cubs aren't dumb. They can quickly change their tactics to escape from someone they think is trying to harm them.

"Craig chased that last cub all over the inside of the pen. He'd get close and the little bear would lunge at him and make scary faces and blow and pop its jaws. I told him to shove the cub into the corner and pick it up by the scruff of the neck.

"He shoved the cub into the corner, but then it balled up on its back with all four feet in the air, claws up. This made it real hard to grab him by the scruff of the neck. The little rascal looked like a bowling ball with claws.

"Craig decided to try to nudge it with his foot to roll it over, but when he did that, the bear sprang up off the floor and wrapped around his lower leg with all four paws and held on for dear life.

"Craig started screaming this high pitched scream like he was being eaten alive. He ran to the door of the holding pen screaming, 'Let me out! Let me out!'

"I said, 'I can't let you out with a bear on your leg! You've gotta get control of the bear first, then I'll let you out!'

"All he had to do was reach down and grab the cub by the scruff of the neck, but he was completely hysterical and couldn't do it. I knew the cub might do serious damage if he didn't get it under control, so I went in and snatched the bear off his leg."

After the incident, Craig was referred to as *Griz*, short for Grizzly Bear.

One season in the Smokies was enough for Griz. He landed a master's degree research project studying deer as part of the Florida panther project. We were happy and proud for Griz. He was on his way to a great career as a wildlife biologist.

Then one day at the office, I got a very sad and shocking call from Dr. Joe Clark at the University of Tennessee. Something terrible had happened. Craig had been involved in an airplane crash in Florida while tracking wildlife in his study. Craig and the pilot of the small aircraft were trying to get a location fix on one of the radio-collared animals, and while circling in a tight pattern to get an exact location, the plane accidentally stalled and crashed. There were no survivors.

Bill Stiver and I went to Craig's funeral. I still get a lump in my throat, even now as I'm writing this. Griz was a great person who loved people and wildlife. He was a person everyone wanted to have around. He was a funny guy who found humor in just about everything. I'm so glad we had the chance to know and work with Griz, even for a short time. He was bound and determined to have a career as a wildlife biologist and he would've made a good one.

We love you and miss you Griz.

HUNGRY AS A BEAR

ENCOUNTERS WITH BEARS don't always go well. It's rare, especially considering the millions of people who visit the Park, but every so often a tourist gets into a potentially deadly situation with a bear.

Sometimes it's totally innocent and accidental, like when a hiker comes around a bend in a trail and suddenly realizes they've unintentionally gotten too close to a bear, startling the animal and themselves. But usually the problems are caused when a person intentionally walks up close to an animal to take a photo or to get a better look.

The worst cases are when people use food to entice a wild animal to approach them. If they're successful, they've probably reduced the bear's lifespan or caused its death. They've taught the bear something that will force us to relocate it or worse, euthanize it.

The person who entices the bear with food may survive the encounter, but the next person who comes along, not suspecting that a hungry wild animal has been taught to see people as a potential source of food can then find themselves in a scary, or even deadly, situation through no fault of their own. That's why it's very important for all Park visitors to remember that feeding a bear can lead to it seriously hurting someone.

The *rarest* type of encounter with a bear in the Park is when it appears that the visitor wasn't at fault in the incident and it appears that the bear was behaving like a predator toward a human being. These confrontations are deeply troubling. We might think we know what led to such an incident, but sometimes we can't be sure about why a bear follows or approaches a person.

In 2004 a man jogging down the Tremont Road had a very serious encounter with a bear. As he ran down the gravel road during daylight, a bear popped out of the woods behind him and started chasing him. He knew how to respond to a bear encounter and he did all the right things. He shouted and threw rocks and sticks, but the bear came right up to him in a very aggressive manner.

Over and over the man tried to move away, but the bear repeatedly closed the distance and had to be run off by the man stopping, turning to face the bear, shouting, making himself look as large as possible, and throwing things. This continued until a family driving along the road happened to see the encounter. In an effort to help the man, they pulled close enough so that he could jump onto their vehicle and ride a safe distance away from the animal. The man was extremely fortunate that these people came to his rescue. If they hadn't, things could have ended much worse.

This makes it clear that the bear wasn't afraid to pursue a human, at least not at this time and place. This is a highly unusual and very dangerous situation. It appeared that the bear wasn't after the man's food, but rather was after the man himself. As soon as the jogger was able to reach a ranger station he reported the incident, and we quickly developed a plan to try to locate and capture this particular bear among the dozens of animals living in the area.

We decided to monitor the site and set live culvert traps during the daytime only. Most bears are active at night and, since it's rare for a bear to be active along a road during the day, we felt our best chance to catch the bear responsible for this encounter was during daylight.

We set our traps and started patrolling the road. After three days, we captured a bear in the same location where the man was attacked. We kept the bear at the Wildlife Building for several days while we continued to set traps and walk in the area. No other bears were seen so we felt we had the bear responsible for the attack on the jogger.

We described the situation to the Superintendent, and the decision was made to put the bear down. We have to be severe in situations like this. We do it because it's the best way to protect people and the rest of the bear population. Euthanizing the very few aggressive bears protects humans and the rest of the bears. It prevents the dangerous animals from teaching other bears its bad habits or passing along aggressive tendencies to any more offspring.

The bear's motive was simple—to get food. That's perfectly natural and there's nothing wrong with that. We all have to eat to survive. It's possible that a few bears, when they're starving or otherwise stressed, will look at us as a potential source of food. All the stars have to line up for this to happen, but sometimes they do.

Let me emphasize that predatory behavior of black bears toward humans is extremely rare in the Smokies, or anywhere, especially in the lower forty-eight states. But I assume bears can have bad days just like people do. Let's just hope no one is around when that happens.

These attacks and bear behaviors weighed heavily on my mind. I felt responsible for negative encounters between people and wildlife in the Park. A bear may sometimes look at a person as a potential source of food and exhibit predatory behavior. But we can't predict when this behavior will occur and there's nothing we can do to prevent it.

All we can do is educate people about how to deal with bear encounters. But, even then, we know that might not be enough.

BEAR IN MIND

I OFTEN WONDER what bears are thinking, but I don't really know, even after more than thirty years of working with them. For example, I wish I knew the motive of bears that follow people down a trail.

Some may want a free snack, some might be curious. I'm never sure what's going on in their heads. The worst case scenario would be that bears are evaluating us as a possible prey species. Fortunately for hikers, campers, or anyone who enjoys the outdoors, predation from bears almost never occurs.

But it has happened a few times in the past and will surely happen again in the future. We just don't know when that next time will be.

One summer on the Old Sugarlands Trail on a Sunday afternoon, an elderly couple, a man and his wife, were hiking toward Cherokee Orchard Road along a slight incline on what used to be an old gravel road when a ninety-pound female bear suddenly approached them. The bear emerged from thick vegetation beside the trail and came right up to the couple in a very aggressive mode and with little warning.

The people did everything right. They yelled, screamed, kicked at the bear, and hit her with sticks. They were fighting for their lives, but the bear just wouldn't give up. Thinking the bear might be after their food—and as a last resort—they set their pack on the ground and moved away from it. The man said he believed he could fight the bear better without the pack on.

The bear immediately went to the pack and started rummaging through it. The couple quickly and quietly moved up the trail away from the bear. After a few moments they looked back and saw the bear charging up the trail toward them. Now, *this* is a very serious situation and anything, and I mean *anything*, can happen.

At this point it was pretty clear that the bear wasn't after the couple's food. It was after *them*. Their lives were in serious danger. The bear got *way* too close to them again and they had to fight it off by yelling and screaming and throwing rocks. The man, who did the majority of the fighting, kept his wife behind him to protect her.

The bear was very persistent, but eventually the couple was able to fight her off again and hike on up the trail to their vehicle. They located a ranger and reported the attack. Heath Soehn and another ranger went to the area and discovered the bear was still there. They photographed the bear, then Heath shot it with a beanbag to chase it away.

The rangers retrieved what was left of the couple's pack and belongings. Park Dispatch called me at home and provided me with the details. Warning signs were immediately posted to advise hikers who passed through the area that a bear was active nearby.

The next morning Rick Varner and I went up to see if we could locate the bear. The attack had occurred on a part of the trail where head-high rhododendron lined both sides of an old road. Beyond the shrubs were tall trees that formed the forest overstory.

We wanted to see if we could attract that same bear, so Rick started frying some bacon and putting good smells into the air. Our plan was to wait and see if anything appeared. Thinking this might be an all-day event, I told Rick I'd go out and get us some lunch and would be back soon. I wasn't gone very long.

When I returned, Rick said he was done. *Done*, I wondered. What could that mean?

Rick said a bear showed up soon after I left. He said he opened the culvert trap, baited it, and in no time, the bear walked into the trap and took the bait, causing the door to slam down. She was no longer a threat to our Park visitors.

Based on pictures of the bear taken the previous day by Heath and the other ranger, the bear in the trap appeared to be the right size. Rick said the bear showed up and began walking around, circling him, and watching him intently.

Was this the same bear?

Well, even though a person was frying bacon, wild bears wouldn't normally approach a human and behave like this one did. Was she after the bacon, or was she after Rick? We couldn't know for sure.

It was highly unusual for a Park bear to be exhibiting such aggressive behavior, though. It was particularly odd to have shown up so quickly in the same area where the attack had occurred, and in the daytime. Normally, wild bears don't act this way. We believed this had to be the same animal that had stalked the elderly couple the day before.

We loaded everything into the truck and towed the trap back to the Wildlife Building. We kept the animal for a few days and at the same time we monitored the area where Rick had captured it. Frying bacon every day didn't draw any other bears to the site, though, so we felt confident we had the correct bear.

We described the events to the Superintendent and he agreed that the best and safest action for our visitors and for the Smokies bear population was to euthanize this bear. We euthanized it by lethal injection using techniques approved by the American Veterinary Medical Association.

Whenever we have to put a bear down, I feel like I've failed in some way. I had no knowledge about the history of this bear, no idea what she'd previously gone through that could've caused her to behave in this manner. We'll never know the reason she got so aggressive. Putting her down wasn't a pleasant part of my job. I know it was the right thing to do, but it still made for a terrible day.

Was the bear predatory? Yes, I think so, because of how she reacted when the couple laid their pack down. Does that worry me? Yes, it does.

Was there an obvious reason this bear acted predatory to the couple? No, not that we know of. And *that* worries me most of all. The bear appeared to have decided spontaneously to view human beings as food and that's extremely scary. What if this incident had involved a small person hiking alone? What if they'd decided to run from the bear, and not stand and fight her?

We could've had a totally different outcome and it might not have been good.

THE BAT CAVE

WE'VE DONE A LOT of heavy, dirty labor building fences to protect people, wild critters, plants, and historic structures. We've constructed all sorts of elaborate cages and fences to keep bears, elk, wolves, and deer from causing havoc. Sometimes we've fenced animals *in*, and sometimes we've fenced them *out*.

Several times we've had to go outside the Park to build fences to protect people's livestock or gardens from species we were trying to reintroduce into the area, like elk and wolves. When dealing with animals, this has usually worked out well. But the most difficult predators to deal with are *humans*.

The spelunkers are particularly tough to deter. There are several caves in the Park, including the deepest cave in Tennessee. Entering some of these caves is strictly forbidden for various excellent reasons, but it doesn't seem to matter to certain kinds of people.

One of the of the most labor intensive days I ever experienced was the day we built a gate at the entrance to Blow Hole Cave at White Oak Sinks. This cave is located off Laurel Creek Road on the way to Cades Cove. The U.S. Fish and Wildlife Service and the National Park Service were very concerned about intrusions into this cave because it holds the largest hibernacula of endangered Indiana bats in Tennessee. Hibernacula is Latin for *tent for winter quarters*.

We knew that we had to increase our protection of these bats because a lot of spelunkers were going into the cave during the winter. Their intrusion was disturbing the hibernating bats, waking them up, and making them use up their energy reserves. Cavers were killing the bats by causing them to starve to death during their hibernation period.

The U.S. Fish and Wildlife Service asked us to build a monstrosity of a gate at the entrance to the cave to try to save the endangered bats. The barrier was built strong enough to hold an elephant or a rhinoceros at bay. It had to be extremely heavy-duty because some of the spelunkers are persistent vandals who will carry in hydraulic jacks so they can spread gate bars wide enough apart for them to squeeze through.

The construction site was about two miles off Laurel Creek Road, and we had to travel nearly half that distance on foot. That meant we had to carry in all the supplies we needed: concrete, large pieces of angle iron, welders, cutting torches, mixing tools, acetylene, and oxygen tanks.

We hand-carried about 11,000-pounds of gear that day. That's five and a half tons. We had to walk about three-fourths of a mile each way, on an extremely hot, humid day, during a heavy downpour of rain. Walking along the trail was like wading through a creek. It was hard going in conditions that made for blistered feet and ruined boots.

It wasn't a pleasant day, but we got the job done, and we kept the bats as safe from the cavers as we could. The gate we built still stands to keep intruders out. But now the bats face another major threat: white nose syndrome.

Over six million North American bats have been killed by this disease, named for a white fungus that can be seen on the afflicted bats. We hope research will provide some answers that will help deal with this dreadful disease and prevent the loss of these endangered creatures.

Contrary to what many people think, bats are good for the environment. A single bat can eat up to a thousand mosquitoes an hour. Multiply that times thousands of bats per cave and it means that hundreds of tons of insects are eaten every night. Bats may not be the most beautiful or majestic wild animal on the earth, but they serve an important role in nature.

BAD DAY FOR ELK

ELK ONCE ROAMED along the Tennessee-North Carolina border, but they were wiped out through over-hunting and loss of habitat. The last elk still living in North Carolina was believed to have been killed in the late 1700s. The last elk in Tennessee was killed in the mid-1800s. By 1900, the population of elk in North America had dropped to the point where hunting and conservation organizations became worried the species was headed for extinction.

One of the primary missions of the National Park Service is to preserve the native plants and animals and attempt to restore lost species on the lands it manages. In the Smokies we'd already been successful at reintroducing the river otter, peregrine falcon, and three species of fish, so eventually we became interested in trying to reestablish larger animals.

In the late 1990s we decided to try to reintroduce elk to the Park. Project partners included the Great Smoky Mountains National Park, Rocky Mountain Elk Foundation, Parks Canada, U.S. Forest Service at Land Between the Lakes, Great Smoky Mountains Association, Friends of the Smokies, U.S. Geological Survey Biological Resources Division, and the University of Tennessee.

The experimental release of elk into the Park began in February of 2001 with the importation of twenty-five animals from the Land Between the Lakes National Recreation Area, which is located along the Tennessee-Kentucky border. Then in 2002, we brought in another twenty-seven animals from Elk Island National Park, Alberta, Canada.

We put radio collars on the elk and monitored them for eight years. We worked hard to manage the big critters. It wasn't easy. Several of the worst days I ever had at work were when our elk got into trouble roaming outside the Park. One of the toughest days was when I got a call about nuisance elk coming onto Charlie Jones' property and went to talk with him about it.

Charlie Jones was a good guy, a hard worker, and a part-time farmer. He kept a few cattle on a small farm on the side of a hill in the White Oak community in North Carolina, near I-40 mile marker 17. The Interstate ran adjacent to his property. Two of our elk had showed up at his farm and he was very upset about it.

Elk #9 and her calf had decided they liked the Jones place, but his cattle had never seen elk before and they were afraid of them. I don't think the elk meant any harm, but the cows weren't coping well with the funny-looking newcomers.

Elk are social and like to play. Some cattle are able to tolerate this, but others aren't. If a cow runs from an elk, some elk will chase it, wanting to play. Elk #9 and her calf were spooking Charlie's animals.

Charlie worked the night shift at a trucking company. He needed to sleep during the day. The elk were causing problems when he was trying to sleep. I understood why he was upset and I wanted to help him as much as I possibly could.

The call I got was because the elk had frightened his cows so severely they'd broken through a fence and run across the road. When I got there it was just after dark. Charlie was really angry and behaved very loud and aggressive toward me.

"I wanna call the sheriff," he said, "I wanna see a lawyer. I'll kill these animals. I'm sick and tired of em and I'm not gonna put up with this." I could see he carried a lot of anger and resentment. He really chewed me out, and repeated, "I wanna *kill* em."

I apologized to him for the situation. I told him I understood how he felt. I grew up on a farm myself and we raised cattle. I remembered how unpleasant it was when the cows got out—trying to find them, herding them back into their pasture, searching until you discovered where they got out, and then fixing the fence.

I felt terrible that Charlie's cows were frightened into stampeding through their fences. I wanted to do my best to help him. But darting and moving a mother elk and calf would take some time. I had to find them and get set up for a good shot. I couldn't guarantee that I could do that in a few hours. I'd probably need a few days, but Charlie wasn't in the mood to give me more time. He wanted the elk gone tomorrow.

Charlie kept chewing me out telling me he wanted to kill the elk. He wanted something done immediately. He didn't seem to have any flexibility about a solution. I didn't have the option of darting the elk and relocating them because Charlie was in such a hurry to have them gone.

I finally realized nothing was going to change his mind. The elk had to go, one way or the other.

Reluctantly, I said, "I'll come back tomorrow and shoot em, Charlie. I'll get em off your property."

I left at 10 p.m. feeling extremely dejected.

On the drive back home I stopped to get a sandwich at Arby's in Newport. It was a little after midnight when I called my wife, Donna, at home. We'd met in high school and married young. She said, "Where are you?"

I told her I was sitting in back of the Arby's parking lot trying to pull myself together. I told her I'd just had one of the worst days of my career. I explained that I'd done my best to resolve the elk problem for Mr. Jones, but it hadn't been good enough.

I was in a major struggle trying to protect the few elk we had in North Carolina in the hope that we could establish a population for people to enjoy in the future. But, at the same time, I wanted to protect the North Carolina landowners and their interests as well.

Lots of people wanted elk brought back to North Carolina, but not *everyone* did, and Charlie was one of the ones who didn't.

I liked to think of myself a problem solver, but it didn't look like I was going to be able fix this situation. Mr. Jones was too upset with me, the Park, and the elk. His ranting and raving had really beaten me down. I just wanted to crawl in a hole and stay there for a while.

"Come on home," Donna said, "and get some sleep. You'll feel better tomorrow."

I went home, but I didn't sleep very well because the next day I was going to have to go back to Mr. Jones' place to kill the elk cow and her calf. I dreaded it.

In the morning I went to the Wildlife Building and got our 30.06, a high-powered hunting rifle. This was the same type of gun that was used by the military in World Wars I and II, Korea, Vietnam, and up to the present.

Rick Varner and I carefully practice-fired it at a target and adjusted the gun sight to be sure the rifle was going to shoot where I was aiming. Rick is an expert on guns and I wanted him to make sure everything was adjusted perfectly. When I shot the mother elk and calf, I wanted it to be a quick, clean, and humane kill. I didn't want either of the animals to suffer.

Before I left Park Headquarters, I contacted Mike Carraway, a wildlife technician with the North Carolina Wildlife Resources Commission. I explained the situation and told him that I felt the best way to solve the problem at Mr. Jones' place was to shoot both of the elk. I was pretty depressed about the whole situation.

Mike made some calls and got this action approved. I also discussed the situation with the Park Superintendent and got his concurrence. Now that the gun was sighted in and everything was approved, I couldn't delay what had to come next. I told Mr. Jones

I'd be at his house at 1 p.m. Mike said he'd meet me there.

As I made the hour-and-a-half drive from Gatlinburg to Mr. Jones' farm, I felt like I'd failed. I knew there were a lot of people who were hoping the elk program would be a success. For that to happen, we needed to retain every elk. Cows were particularly important in building a sustainable population. Today we were going to lose two of our elk and both of them were females.

I drove slowly up the driveway to the Jones house. I could see Mike and Charlie sitting out front on the porch. I was ready for Round 2 with Charlie and expected another terrible encounter. My hide was getting thicker, though, so I was prepared to accept another tongue-lashing.

As I got out of the truck, I heard Charlie say, "Kim come up here. I wanna talk to you."

I thought to myself, *Great, I'm gonna get it again.* But then I realized something about the tone of Charlie's voice was different. As I walked up onto the porch, I looked at him. He didn't seem like the same person I'd talked to the night before.

Had I missed something? I was confused, but had no idea what to expect next. Charlie looked at me, and said, "Set down here for just a second. I need to tell you something."

I did as I was told.

"I need to apologize for the way I treated you last night," he said, "I was very disrespectful."

"It's okay," I said.

"No, it's *not* okay," he said in a very stern tone. "My mom and wife and daughter told me I owed you an apology and they're right. I was very, very disrespectful to you. Let me tell you why I talked to you like I did."

I was shocked at the change in his behavior, but I sat still, listening.

"Son," Charlie said, "when I was growin up I loved to bear hunt more than just about anything. When my dogs started chasin a bear near my house, guess where the bear ran to?"

"The Park," I said.

As the crow's flies, Charlie's farm wasn't far from the Park boundary. It wouldn't take long for a running bear to reach the protection of the National Park, especially if it was being chased by a pack of barking dogs.

"That's right," Charlie said. "Most of the bears I was chasin during a hunt ran right into the Park. That meant I had to drive over to Cataloochee to pick up my dogs. Usually, by the time I got there, a ranger or a visitor had picked up the dogs and was holdin em in a kennel until the owner could come pick em up. I'll never forget those meetings with the rangers.

"I was treated like a criminal or an outlaw. I was treated very disrespectful. I dreaded havin to go over there to get my dogs because I knew what was gonna happen. Every time I had to do it, I'd get madder and more upset. I got sick and tired of being treated like a second-class person when I hadn't done anything wrong.

"I was huntin legally. I couldn't help it if my dogs ignored the Park boundary signs. Since then, I've had a hatred for the government, and the National Park in particular. My treatment at the hands of the Park rangers made me so angry I even stopped bear huntin. I vowed I'd never set foot in the Park again or take my kids there, ever, and I haven't.

"Now do you see why I acted like I did when a so-called government elk came onto my land? It was because of the way I was treated by the Park rangers when I was growin up. I don't blame you for these elk being here. You're just doin your job."

The way Charlie had treated me the night before was starting to make sense. He wasn't really mad at me or the elk. His anger was directed toward Park rangers from the past and I just happened to be in the wrong place at the wrong time when he vented some of that bottled up anger.

"Charlie," I said, "I can't change the past. I'm sorry you were treated that way. It was wrong."

I reminded him that his bad experience happened long before I started working for the Park and told him that I didn't know any of the people who'd been rangers then. I tried to reassure him that I knew the current Cataloochee rangers and they were good people. We sat looking at each other.

Finally, he said, "Do you think you can dart those elk?"

I couldn't believe what I was hearing. Less than twenty-four hours before, he'd made me promise to kill both the mother and her calf. But now it looked like it this might be their lucky day.

"Yeah," I said, "I think so. I believe I can catch em, but it might take me three or four days."

Charlie sat there for a minute and then said, "Okay, then. Go ahead and dart the cow and take her back to the Park. If you have trouble catchin the calf, just leave it. It'll take up with my cattle. You can come back later and get it."

I was in shock. I couldn't believe what had just happened. It was a huge relief, though. I shook his hand, thanked him, and left. The women in his family, his mother and wife and daughter, had changed everything. They'd saved the lives of the two elk. If elk could talk, I know they'd give a big thanks to those ladies.

A couple of days later I drove by with Jennifer Murrow, an elk researcher who was working on her Ph.D. We found Elk #9 and her calf standing close to the road. As soon as we saw her, I called Rick Varner and asked him to bring the elk trailer over. We drove on past the two elk, stopped the Ford Explorer along the side of the road, and prepared a dart for the 600-pound cow.

When I had everything ready, I crossed Charlie's fence, and slowly eased over the hill close to where the mother elk and her calf were standing. I looked through my rangefinder. She was thirty-five yards away.

I carefully placed the 1.5 cc dart in the gun and closed the lever. Next, I worked the bolt to place a .22 caliber blank into the chamber. Then I dialed the power setting to position #3 which is typically used for a thirty-five yard shot. Finally, I raised the dart gun, placed the crosshairs on the mother elk's hindquarter, and squeezed the trigger.

A crack similar to the sound of firing a .22 pistol sounded. The dart flew downhill and into the elk's hip. When it hit, a small pop and flash from the dart revealed that the drug had been injected into the animal. The mother elk bolted and ran down the hill, then stopped to look back at me.

Five minutes later she was lying on the ground snoozing. Soon afterwards, Rick arrived with the elk trailer. We rolled her onto a strong, six-foot-by-eight-foot tarp, specially made with handles around the edges. Rick had brought along an ATV that pulled a small two-wheeled trailer. Using the tarp, we maneuvered the elk onto the little trailer. Then Rick towed the elk over to the large trailer.

We slid the elk into the big trailer, I injected the reversal drugs, and we closed the back gate. Within ten minutes, the mother elk was standing up and looking around. Her 275-pound calf had moved away and was hiding in some thick brush, peeking out at us. I don't think either of the elk was pleased about what had just happened.

We hauled Elk #9 to a small field near the Oconaluftee Visitor Center just outside Cherokee, North Carolina. That's a little over fifteen miles from the Jones farm. This was the farthest I'd ever moved an elk within the Park. I was hoping this was far enough that she wouldn't be tempted to go back over to Charlie's farm.

A couple of days later Bill Stiver and I went back to the Jones place looking for the calf. When we found it, I loaded up a dart, made a short stalk to get within forty yards, and fired the rifle. Fortunately the dart found its mark and we soon had the one-year-old calf in the trailer heading over to Oconaluftee to reunite it with its mother.

There was about an hour left before dark when we arrived at the field where a small group of elk were feeding. I looked through my binoculars and, sure enough, there stood Elk #9, the mother of the calf we had in the trailer.

All of the elk were watching us intently as we opened the door. The calf ran out of the trailer, stopped, and did a double take at the group of elk. Then the calf walked directly toward the herd. At the same time the mother elk walked toward her calf, and they were soon reunited in the middle of the field where the mother sniffed the calf from head to toe.

I called and thanked Charlie for his understanding in letting us move the elk. I also asked him to thank his mother and wife and daughter. I told Charlie that things had changed in the Park since he was mistreated and suggested he make a trip to Cataloochee to see the elk.

"I don't know," he said.

Later that year, in early fall, Jennifer Murrow, who'd helped me dart the mother elk at the Jones farm, called and said, "You won't believe who I saw in Cataloochee—Charlie Jones! He was there on a picnic with his church!"

Jennifer was so pleased to see him in the Park she went up and talked to him. It was a good reunion for both Charlie and the Park. So what started out as a bad situation, a terrible situation, had a happy ending all the way around.

Even though things worked out well in the end, I'll always remember that terrible night and how quickly things can change. I'd acquired a thicker hide and learned that sometimes it really pays to listen.

THE BEST LAID PLANS

FRED FARLEY IS A PLANNER for the Park who works in the Maintenance Division. He creates planning documents for Park roads, retaining walls, bridges and other engineering or construction projects. He's also a hunter who's intrigued with wildlife management.

He'd often say, "Y'all have the greatest job in the world!"

One afternoon, when I was in my office at Headquarters, I got a call on the radio from Dispatch saying, "There's a bear on the Sugarlands Nature Trail. It's sitting in the middle of the trail, not letting people pass, and you can see him from the road, so it's causing a traffic jam on Hwy. 441, too."

"Okay," I said, "I'll go take care of it."

Fred happened to be passing by my office and heard my conversation with Dispatch.

"What's going on?" he said. I told him I had to go deal with a bear on the Sugarlands Nature Trail. "Can I go with you?" he asked.

When you respond to any bear call, it's always good to have someone with you, because you never know what might happen. So I said, "Well, yeah, sure you can. The more the merrier."

I put on my Park Service ball cap, picked up my radio, and went out the door.

"You're not gonna take anything?" Fred said.

I shook my head.

"What're you gonna do?"

"We're gonna move the bear outta the trail and away from the road," I said, as I headed toward the Nature Trail at a fast walk.

"No, *really*," Fred said, "what *exactly* are we gonna do?"

"I don't *exactly* know Fred."

We walked for another minute and he asked again, "I mean like, what do you *think* you might do?"

He was walking sideways trying to make eye contact, but I had my head down and was trying to focus on where I was going.

"I don't have a plan," I said. "I'm just responding to a call."

"But what if we get there and we can't run it off? What happens if it charges you? Tell me what you're thinking."

"I'm not thinking," I said, "I'm just responding!"

Fred was a professional planner who took action based on a well thought out process. This is, of course, the best way to approach most situations. But, in wildlife management, it's a little different. We've learned the hard way that we have to show up at the site of the problem, evaluate the situation when we get there, and *then* try to formulate some type of solution.

The fourth time Fred asked me what I might do when we reached the bear, I stopped and looked at him as if I was dead serious, although I wasn't. I said, "Okay, I give up. I'll tell you the plan. The plan is this: if we get up there and we try to chase that bear off and it charges toward us, I'm gonna pick up the biggest stick I can find, turn around, and hit you square in the knee with it, and then I'm gonna run off as fast as I can go."

I gave Fred a totally fake stern look.

He looked back at me in surprise and confusion, and said, "Why would you do that?"

"Because I'm fifty-four years old and a little heavy for my height," I said, "so I can't run as fast as I did in my younger years. You're younger, thinner, and in better shape than me, so I'm betting you're much faster, especially when you're scared. You know the old joke about how to survive a bear attack: *Make sure you hike with someone who you can outrun.*

Fred looked stricken, so I admitted I was just kidding and told him again that I honestly had no plan whatsoever. Fred was quiet after that, but I could tell he was disappointed.

We soon got to where the bear was sitting. When we saw it, Fred stopped on the trail and I continued walking. I jumped toward the bear, waved my hands in the air, yelled, shuffled my feet in the leaves, and threw a couple of rocks. I'm sure I looked like a maniac to Fred. Apparently the bear thought so too, because he ran off into the woods.

That was it. I did my job with no plan, no meetings, no strategy sessions. I just waved, shouted, acted crazy, threw some rocks, and I was done!

Fred remained subdued. I could tell his ideas about the glamorous and adventurous life of a wildlife ranger had been crushed. He was silent as we walked back to Park Headquarters. When we reached my office, he forced a weak smile and lifted his hand in a half-hearted wave, then he continued toward his own office, shaking his head and mumbling to himself.

PLAYING ALL THE TIME

IF I HAD TO CHOOSE AN ANIMAL to come back as after I die, it would be a river otter. They seem to play all the time.

Otters used to be common in east Tennessee. But by the 1930s, when the Park was first created, they were almost all gone. Humans are the main predator of river otters. The critters were virtually wiped out by trappers who wanted their pelts.

Then fifty years later, in 1986, the Park began an otter reintroduction program. After the Tennessee Wildlife Resources Agency released some river otters near Crossville, Tennessee, we decided to try it, too.

The program was set up as an experiment. We didn't know if otters could stand our cold mountain water or if they could catch enough fish to survive in our fast moving streams. We got eleven river otters from North Carolina and chose Abrams Creek for our first release because there aren't many swimmers or tubers in that area.

Jane Griess at the University of Tennessee was in charge of research for the otter reintroduction. Veterinarians at the university surgically implanted a small, oblong radio transmitter just underneath the otters' hide, near the stomach. The battery would last about a year and a half and the little transmitters wouldn't cause any problems for the animals.

Before all the otters had been operated on, one of them escaped from a holding facility on a farm across the river from the vet school. On the day the otter got out, the ground was covered with snow so it was easy to follow its path. The otter's tracks meandered around the area near the building where the group was held, then indicated a straight line slide down the hill to the big river. We never knew where that otter chose to make his new home.

Once the ten remaining otters were ready to go, we released them from Abrams Falls parking area on the west end of Cades Cove. Most of them stayed in the Abrams Creek drainage area. There were only two *flyers*, as we called the ones that left the Park. One of them went all the way to Tellico Lake near Vonore. The other died in Chilhowee Lake after being caught in a fishing net.

The reintroduction was controversial with some of the local fishermen. They worried that the otters might eat all the trout. But we felt relatively safe trying to reestablish the animals because research indicated that otters preferred more slow-moving prey like suckers or crayfish. This proved to be the case in the Smokies.

Crayfish remains were found in ninety percent of the otter *scat*, or droppings. We learned that during the month of January, however, when crayfish were less available, otters would search for any fish to eat, and catch trout or catfish that were confined to small streams or ponds.

A couple of years later, in 1988, we got fourteen more otters from South Carolina and Louisiana and released them into Little River near Elkmont. We tried Little River because we wanted to see if otters could make it in places that were heavily used by people, such as where there were swimmers, tubers, and fishermen, as well as kids hollering and throwing rocks, people barbecuing, and cars going by.

They did okay there, too. We noticed that they moved up to higher elevation waters in the summer and then came back down in the winter when the use of the river by Park visitors was greatly reduced. Four years later, in 1992, the reintroduction was declared a success and we switched from otter research to otter management.

We released six more otters into Cataloochee Creek, four into Hazel Creek, and two into Little River. Most of these otters stayed in the Park. But one of them settled in the French Broad River outside the Park, and three of the ones released into Little River crossed the mountains and established their home ranges on the North Carolina side of the Park.

Leroy Sevin, a Louisiana resident and trapper, figured out a way to calm trapped wild otters so they could be moved to other states for reintroduction projects. Leroy provided otters to Missouri, Ohio, Tennessee, and the Park. In one deal, the state of Louisiana was trying to restore wild turkeys, so they traded with the state of Missouri, swapping otters for turkeys.

Then in January of 1994, we learned that Leroy had a hundred wild river otters for sale in Houma, Louisiana for $400 each, so we bought them. The day we brought those hundred otters up from south Louisiana, transporting them in a horse-hauling truck, it was snowing in Greenbrier. We worried the otters would be upset by the cold, but instead, as soon as we released them, they started running and sliding on the snow.

They seemed to be having fun. I'm fairly sure that those otters had never seen snow in their lives, and yet they immediately took the opportunity to play in it, even with us standing there watching them. They had to have been afraid of us and wanted to get away, and yet playfulness is such a part of their nature, they couldn't help themselves.

When the otters first jumped into the cold water, they immediately (and I mean immediately) jumped right back out and shook themselves off in surprise. But then, after that initial shock, they did fine.

The hundred river otters from Louisiana were the last release we made. We turned them loose into the West and Middle Prong of the Little Pigeon River, Oconaluftee River, Big Creek, Cataloochee Creek, Abrams Creek, Little River, Twentymile Creek, Tab Cat Creek, Deep Creek, Eagle Creek, Forney Creek, Pilkey Creek, Chambers Creek, and Noland Creek.

River otters can now be found in most of the waterways around the mountains. They're very popular with visitors who are lucky enough to get to see them swimming and frolicking.

THE DORITO DEER

ONE SUMMER I GOT SEVERAL CALLS from a ranger in Cades Cove complaining that people were feeding deer on the back side of the eleven-mile Cades Cove Loop road near the Visitor Center.

"Why don't you write tickets to stop it?" I said.

"We've written some," he said, "and we'd write more if we could catch the people who're doing it! But we can't always be there."

I understood. They had an impossible job, trying to be everywhere and watch everyone in the cove.

People can be sneaky. Two million of them drive around the Cades Cove Loop road every year. And the ones who're mean enough to feed the animals, are usually smart enough not to feed them when a ranger's around. As a result of being enticed by tourists, the deer were getting hooked on junk food and becoming less afraid of visitors.

"The deer are starting to come up to people," the ranger said. "Can you help us?"

"Okay," I said. "We'll give it a try."

The following day I went to the cove with Claudia, a summer intern with the wildlife department who'd traveled around the world helping with research projects in remote areas. We watched the deer to see which ones were bumming food. My plan was to catch and relocate the ones that were tame enough to walk up to cars to get fed.

There were ten or twelve deer grazing in the field. We watched them for a long time. It was like a stakeout. But while we waited none of the deer made a move toward the Loop road and nobody walked toward the deer to offer them food.

Claudia had a big bag of Doritos and she was eating them while we waited.

I suspected that some visitors might've been feeding the deer with potato chips. I asked Claudia for her bag of Doritos and pulled the *Sow* truck to the edge of road near the small herd of deer. I rolled the window down, stuck the bag out, and rattled it as loudly as possible.

All of the deer jerked their heads up and looked our way. Then, almost immediately, one of them began to walk toward us. The deer recognized the sound, so now we knew for sure that people had been feeding them out of bags. Deer would be interested in potato chips because they're salty. We believe deer and elk may have trouble finding enough salt in the mountains.

One of the deer walked straight up to us. I couldn't believe it. I fumbled around hurriedly, getting my drugs and darts together. Then I got my rifle ready, but by then I had to shoo the deer away because it was too close to shoot! When the deer moved back far enough, I fired a dart into its rear quarter. After four or five minutes the animal fell fast asleep, and we loaded it into a four-by-four-by-eight-foot deer transfer cage, which is a wooden box with holes in it.

Since the strategy worked so well the first time, I decided to try the same technique again. I rattled the Doritos bag and here came another deer. It walked straight toward our vehicle, and came right up to us as I was crinkling the bag. I darted that one, too, and loaded it into the transfer cage.

While we were doing this, the deer herd stayed nearby and watched. I rattled the Doritos bag a third time and all the deer looked my way, but none of them came over. When I'm working with animals, I always wonder what they're thinking. Are they asking themselves and each other, *Does he think we're stupid? I'm not going over there and getting shot with a dart and put in a box!*

We took the two captured deer and released them about ten miles away on the end of Parson Branch Road. After that we never had any more serious problems with deer approaching cars in that area.

We did receive a single sketchy report of a deer sticking its head into a vehicle on Parson Branch Road. Bet you could guess what it was looking for.

THE BEAR THIEF

GRADUALLY OVER THE MONTHS and then years, I gained more and more experience dealing with wildlife. That meant when new guys were hired to help out, they'd sometimes call me for advice when they got into trouble. I was rarely able to offer any specific guidance because every problem with an animal in the back-country tends to be a one-of-a-kind situation, but I guess it helped to have someone to call.

We hired a young fellow, Ray Branson, as a seasonal hog hunter and assigned him to the same area when I'd started out—the high regions of the Park along the Appalachian Trail. Ray was a dedicated woodsman from Pennsylvania. He was a really good guy who I was proud to have as part of our wildlife team. He was stocky, red-haired, hard-working, and honest. And just like I was during my early days, he was a bit afraid of bears.

Hikers had reported that wild hogs were plowing up the ground on the Appalachian Trail near Pecks Corner, so Ray went up there. He made camp at the Park maintenance cabin, a small rustic build-ing downhill from the Pecks Corner Shelter. It was a popular, but remote, area used mainly by the Park's maintenance people when they were doing trail work on the Appalachian Trail.

By the time Ray arrived at the maintenance camp his clothes were soaked with sweat from his hike up the mountain carrying the heavy load of equipment he needed to stay out in the backcountry for a week. He hung his National Park Service shirt on a makeshift clothesline to dry.

He went inside the little cabin and began to cook supper and or-ganize his equipment before he started his night hike to look for wild hogs. He heard something rustling outside and went to the door. He popped his head out just in time to see a large bear loping off into the woods carrying a prize. The bear had snatched Ray's shirt off the clothesline and was gone in a flash.

Ray was extremely upset when he realized what the bear had stolen because the shirt was his official Park Service uniform and it had his badge and nametag pinned to it. Ray was a serious, no-nonsense, professional kind of person and very conscientious about doing the right thing. He called me on the radio and told me what had happened.

"Three-forty, this is three-forty-five," he said, in a very business-like tone of voice. *Three-forty* was my radio code name, *three-forty-five* was Ray's.

"I'm at the maintenance cabin near Pecks," he said. "A bear's run off with my Park Service shirt and I can't find it. What do you advise?"

I was sitting in my office and Bill Stiver happened to be there with me. I turned to Bill and said, "Did he ask me what I would advise?"

Bill nodded *yes*.

I threw my hands in the air as I thought about what to say. All the other Park radio traffic stopped, so I knew everyone was listening to Ray's bear story and waiting to see what advice I'd give him. Of course, I had no idea how he could get his shirt back.

It was a struggle not to laugh at the mental picture I was getting of a bear running away with Ray's National Park Service shirt. I was sure the other Park employees listening to the exchange were amused by the situation, too.

With absolutely no idea of any useful guidance for Ray, I keyed my microphone, and said in the most sober tone I could muster, "Three-forty-five, all I can tell you is to pass the word to hikers and backpackers in the area that if anybody sees a bear wearing a Park Service shirt with a badge and a name tag for Ray Branson, it's probably yours."

There was a long pause, then Ray said, "Three-forty-five, copy," serious as ever.

As soon as I signed off, I got calls from employees all over the Park promising to tell me if they saw any bears wearing a Park Service uniform. Each of these calls ended with a big burst of laughter on the other end of the phone.

I told all of the callers that Ray and I really appreciated their help and concern.

Ray was trying to do the right thing and obviously I was no help. As you might guess, Ray never did recover his shirt, or badge, or name tag, but luckily, we've never received any reports of a bear seen wearing them either.

JAY AND THE BEARS

WE WERE MOVING a family of bears from their winter den in the Smokies to the Big South Fork National River and Recreation Area, northwest of Knoxville, near the Kentucky state line. We were trying to learn the best way to reintroduce bears to new areas.

For many years, the University of Tennessee bear researchers had radio-collared adult females throughout the Park, so we had excellent maps showing us where these momma bears were denned during the winter. On this particular day, we were hoping to work with a bear in a ground den on the side of a steep hill, but the entrance hole was narrow. Only a small person would be able to get in.

It was obvious that none of us, especially me, could possibly squeeze inside to extract the bear. We looked around for a possible candidate. All eyes ended up on Jay Clark.

Jay was a wildlife student and bear researcher earning his B.S. in Wildlife and Fisheries Science. He was the smallest member of the group so he was going to have to go in.

Although he was extremely goosey about bears, and that's putting it mildly, he reluctantly agreed to let us lower him into the den to see if he could get the bear out.

First we reached in with a long jabstick and injected the bear. Then we waited for her to fall asleep. As we waited, Jay was obviously nervous. He wanted to know exactly who would be holding his ankles as he'd be lowered into the deep, dark, underground cavity where he was supposed to grab hold of the sleeping bear—at least we hoped she'd be asleep.

"Listen," he said, "if you let go of me and that bear wakes up and tears my eyes out and rips my ears off, I'll get even with you. That's a promise!"

We carefully lowered Jay through the den opening so he could take hold of the bear. When he was all the way in, he called in a muffled, high-pitched voice, "Pull me out!"

I couldn't resist saying, "What?"

"Pull me outta here *now!*" he shouted.

As we pulled Jay out, we could see his hands were wrapped around some black furry feet. When we had the bear out, too, Jay looked at me with an accusing expression, and said, "When I told you to pull me out, I didn't stutter."

We struggled to hide our smiles as we loaded the bear for transport with Jay mumbling, "Act like they didn't hear me …."

Jay was a hero that day. We couldn't have gotten the bear out without him. And even though he'd been afraid, he'd stepped up when we needed him.

Jay had already gotten famous among the wildlife crew for his early introduction to bears in the Park. It was only his fourth day on the job when I got a call from Dispatch saying that a bear had been hit by a car on the Spur. The Spur is the section of highway that leads to the Park between Pigeon Forge and Gatlinburg.

I called Rick Varner and Jay and asked them if they could respond and try to find the bear and see what condition it was in. It wasn't going to be easy because the incident happened after dark. When Jay and Rick got to the scene of the accident they found skid marks on the road and evidence that a bear had been hit. It looked like the bear had run off into the woods toward the river.

Most people wouldn't want to go into the woods to look for an injured black bear after dark, but Rick isn't afraid of *anything*. Jay was a different story. There was no moon that night, so it was going to be very dark.

Nevertheless someone needed to go after the bear to check on it.

It was the right thing to do. None of us wanted an injured bear to have to lie out in the woods all night long and suffer.

Rick and Jay used the skid marks as a starting point and made their way down the steep bank toward the Little Pigeon River. Then they walked along the riverbank slowly looking for any signs of the bear. They were separated by a few yards when suddenly they heard something moaning and moving beside them in the thick brush.

The sounds were coming from a dark area right between them, and not knowing or caring what it was, they both took off running in opposite directions. Although Jay was farther from the *Elk Calf* pickup truck, had shorter legs, and wasn't nearly as athletic as Rick, Jay reached the vehicle first!

Rick was amazed. "How'd you beat me to the truck?" he said.

"A man's gotta do what a man's gotta do!" said Jay.

That night Jay got a lot more experience with bears than he wanted, and he got it a lot sooner than he expected to. Real life experience comes quickly sometimes.

Rick and Jay realized it wasn't feasible to try to locate and examine the bear in the dark, so they reluctantly gave up their search for the night.

The next morning they returned, but the bear was gone. We assume it healed from its injuries, learned to stay away from the road, and lived a happy life.

REALITY TELEVISION: THE BEAR CHANNEL

BEARS HAVE STRONG HOMING INSTINCTS so it's not always easy to relocate them successfully. We decided to conduct a research project to evaluate the effectiveness of relocating bears during the summer while they were actively foraging versus during the winter when they were hibernating.

When Bill Landry of the *Heartland* television series heard that we were moving black bears from the Park to Big South Fork National River and Recreational Area to try and establish them there, he called and asked to film a backcountry bear capture and release. Bill and his crew had successfully filmed hundreds of shows that focused on the natural and cultural history of the Smokies.

I checked with my supervisor and our public affairs office and they both gave the green light for the *Heartland* crew to tag along. I wasn't comfortable with the idea of a film crew recording every move we made, because I worried something might go wrong. Film crews do a great job and their work is extremely important, but having extra people with us meant more people and more noise. Noise and wild animals don't go together well.

Hiking to a bear den in the backcountry to find a mother bear and her cub, then trying to dart her and carry her and the cub back to a truck, might sound easy when you're just talking about it, but it can be tough, or even impossible, in actual practice. Anything can happen.

Despite my reservations, I notified the *Heartland* crew when we planned to move the bears and they sent three people out to film our little field trip: a cameraman, a sound man, and Bill Landry.

What could go wrong? I wondered.

A male bear is simpler and easier to move than a mother bear with a cub. In fact, there were already a few male bears migrating on their own into Big South Fork from growing populations in Kentucky and Virginia. I should've thought about that before inviting the film crew.

Another complicating factor was that many of the bear dens in the Smokies are inside a hollow cavity in a tree. The entrance to these kinds of dens can be well over fifty feet in the air. This particular bear was sleeping at ground level inside a hollow tree but the entrance hole to the den was way up high.

The sound guy climbed about eighteen feet up a ladder to the den entrance and lowered a microphone down through the hollow tree trunk toward where the mother bear was hibernating. He had headphones on and could hear what was happening inside the den, but he couldn't see anything.

Although the mother bear was sleeping, she had a cub with her that was awake and nursing. It makes a distinctive sound. Bill and the crew wanted to capture these natural sounds from the mother and cub before we lowered the long jabstick into the den and injected the mother with immobilization drugs.

I was sitting on the ground watching the operation unfold, trying to make sure things went well and no one got hurt. Rick Eastridge, a University of Tennessee bear researcher, was standing on a tree limb near the den opening, preparing to inject the mother bear with the pole syringe. The sound guy was at the top of the ladder with headphones on, listening to sounds from the den. The sound guy's assistant was part way up the ladder heavily loaded with recording equipment.

The tree was full of unwelcome visitors to the bear den. The sound guy was looking down, speaking with his assistant who was making some adjustments to their equipment, when he suddenly grabbed his headphones with both hands, and said, "Hey, I think the mother's awake!"

He turned toward the den opening, and said, "I think she's coming out!"

The pitch of his voice went up with each word he spoke. He stuck his head into the opening to take a look, then shouted, "She's coming out *now*!! Oh, %^&*#!!"

He and his assistant were in awkward and vulnerable positions up on a tall ladder, loaded down with delicate and expensive electronic gear. You could see them think about jumping, but with all their equipment one of them was likely to get hurt, hung, or killed. So, both guys descended the twenty-foot ladder, mostly by sliding, using only their hands. I don't think their feet ever touched the steps.

Rick was trying to decide whether he should climb higher in the tree or attempt a giant leap to the ground. After a quick assessment of his options, he jumped out on the uphill side of the tree and landed unharmed. Seeing his acrobatic stunt made me think how nice it would be to be young again.

It was chaos. Everyone scattered. People were running, jumping, falling, and crawling in all directions, trying to get as far away as possible, as fast as possible.

The mother bear came barreling out of the hollow space and leaped downhill away from the tree like a giant flying squirrel. She hit the ground and ran off without looking back.

I had a dart gun with me, but the bear burst out of the den and ran away so fast I couldn't get a shot off. It was a fiasco. The mother bear was young and this was probably her first cub. I'd learned over the years that a young mother black bear wouldn't protect her cubs as much as an older mother would. We were lucky in one sense. Most mother bears would've come after us instead of breaking camp like this bear did.

The three guys who'd been in the tree looked like they'd just had near death experiences. The soundman said it was the scariest moment of his life. The film crew didn't get a single bit of usable footage of anything, the mother bear, the cub, or the mass exodus.

This wasn't how the day was supposed to go, but now we had to pick up the pieces the best we could. Rick and I grabbed our equipment and went after the mother bear. Everyone moved away from the tree in the hope that the mother would come back to get her cub who was now alone.

We searched the area for hours, but found no sign of the mother. She didn't return to the den either. We had to make a decision about whether to leave the cub and hope the mother would come back and get it, or take the cub with us and check the den tomorrow morning to see if the mother had returned.

I seriously doubted she'd return, but if she was there, we'd dart her, carry her out, and reunite her with her cub. If she wasn't, our only option would be to foster the abandoned cub with a new mother. After a quick discussion, we decided the best solution for the cub was to take it with us.

The crew went back to the tree, climbed it again, and extended a long catchpole into the den and carefully removed the little fellow. Leslie Morgan, a wildlife biologist, wrapped the one-pound cub in her scarf and Park Service toboggan. Years earlier Leslie had worked for me, but now she was in charge of the wildlife program at the Big South Fork.

When the cub was ready for travel, everyone hiked out, except for me and the two University of Tennessee student wildlife researchers, Jay Clark and Bob Inman. While I searched along the ridge, Jay and Bob continued to look for the mother bear with their telemetry receiver in a nearby area downhill from the den.

I crossed paths with the film crew and others who were making their way back to the vehicles with the little cub. I asked them if they'd picked up my pack. I'd left it on the ground beside the den tree. They all shook their heads *no*. I was disappointed to learn this. With everything that had happened so far that day, I was dragging, but I had no choice except to hike back and get it.

As we separated, I called Jay on the radio and asked, "Have you guys seen any sign of the mother bear?"

"No," he said.

I told them to call it a day, and said I was going to hike back to the den tree to pick up my backpack. Jay said they'd just left the tree and they were bringing my pack with them. I suggested a good location for us to meet up, and said I'd wait for them there.

I waited in the middle of a rhododendron thicket in a hollow with steep banks on both sides. In a few minutes, I saw Jay and Bob in the distance, coming toward me, working their way downhill through the rhododendron. It had been an exhausting and discouraging day, but I had an irresistible urge to pull a prank, and that gave me energy.

I backed up the hillside and climbed up onto a huge rhododendron bush and lay down on top of it like an overweight cat intending to pounce on some unsuspecting prey. If Jay and Bob followed the old *manway*, an unmaintained trail that ran alongside a small stream, in a few minutes they'd walk directly under me. That's exactly what I was hoping for.

As they approached, I could hear them talking. Jay asked Bob, "Where do you think that mother bear went?"

"I don't know," Bob said, "but I bet we're close to her."

When I heard that, I decided it was the ideal time for me to enter the discussion. The trail underneath me ran alongside a steep, muddy stream bank. By pure coincidence, as Jay was walking under where I was lying, he suddenly slipped and lost his footing and fell onto his back. He lay there facing the overhanging bushes, with the wind knocked out of him. At that exact moment, I started violently shaking the rhododendron bushes above his head and let out the loudest imitation of a bear growl I could muster.

The racket I made would've rivaled Simba's roar when he won his battle over Scar in the movie, *Lion King*. I even scared myself a bit. When I'd exhausted all the air in my lungs, I looked down at Jay and Bob. I wish I had a video of the next ten seconds.

Jay screamed in a less than manly tone, "Oh...... %^&*#!," and started trying to get away as quickly as possible. Unfortunately he made his attempt to escape before standing up or even turning over. He looked like an upside down turtle trying to run a hundred yard dash. His arms were windmilling and his legs were kicking, but he wasn't getting anywhere because he was still lying on his back.

It was a good thing there wasn't actually a bear after him.

Bob leaped backwards in surprise, but his reaction was nowhere near as dramatic as Jay's. When no bear jumped out of the bushes and no further animal sounds were heard, it became quiet for a few moments. Then Jay realized he'd been tricked.

He flopped back down flat on the ground, and said, "I'm sure glad my momma didn't hear me say that."

After we'd all had a good laugh, I apologized to Jay and Bob for tricking them. Neither of them said anything, so I don't believe they forgave me. Anyway, I knew that *what goes around comes around*, so I expected in the future to get repaid with interest for my prank.

That night we used an eyedropper to feed the little cub a milk supplement. He ate well, so he was in good hands for the moment. The next day we checked the den tree. There was still no mother bear to be found. Fortunately, we had another mother bear with two cubs we were holding at the Wildlife Building awaiting transport to Big South Fork.

We decided to place the orphan cub with this family group. The next day we hauled the mother bear and all three cubs to Big South Fork to a ground den under a large rocky overhang.

We sedated the mother and carefully placed her in the den. Then we smeared Vaseline on the back of each cub to try to mask any human smell on them. We hoped the mother would wake up and lick the cubs to clean them. Then, after she licked them off, she wouldn't be able to tell which ones were hers and which one was the orphan.

We nestled the three cubs in the den beside the mother bear and covered the opening with brush. The next spring Leslie Morgan reported seeing the family group out and moving around together, getting accustomed to their new home.

This was a happy ending to a story that didn't start out very well. But I don't think it's purely a coincidence that shortly afterwards I noticed my hair was beginning to turn white.

THE PLACEBO EFFECT

THE DRUGS WE USE TO IMMOBILIZE large, dangerous, wild animals are extremely powerful. You have to be very careful when handling them, so you don't accidentally give yourself or someone else a dose of it, because if you did, it could be deadly.

Carfentanil, the drug we use to immobilize elk, is at least 10,000 times more potent than morphine. A single drop of it is enough to kill eighty people.

A vial of the immobilization drug costs $500. That's enough to capture about a dozen elk. A vial of the drug required to reverse the effects of the immobilization and get the elk back up on their feet costs $600. The drugs are expensive, but well worth it. It's amazing to be able to subdue a 700-pound elk with a three-inch dart and twenty drops of medicine.

When I dart an elk and things go well, it takes about four to five minutes for the elk to go down. Then we can move in close to the animal and do whatever we need to do. We often work at dusk because the elk come out of the woods into the meadows. All the jostling around with a heavy animal in the dark can result in accidents and things can suddenly get dicey. This happened once when we were working on an elk at Cove Creek outside the Cataloochee area of the Park.

It was spring and we had a five-by-five-point bull elk that had gotten too close to some local residents' pets and ornamental shrubs. We decided to catch him and move him to Oconaluftee, or Luftee as it's sometimes called. Luckily I had two of our best wildlife rangers with me, Bill Stiver and Sam Hillerman.

Bill worked with me at Park Headquarters. Sam was stationed in the Cataloochee area working primarily on elk, but he did all kinds of wildlife work. Sam was an employee you never had to worry about. He always seemed to make the right decisions. We were fortunate he was part of our wildlife team.

The three of us and several helpers headed out in the *Boar* truck late in the day, set up our equipment, and waited, hoping to see the elk. Sure enough, the bull we were looking for popped out into a small field. I worked my way around the animal to get into position. When the elk finally moved close enough to me, I took the shot and the small dart landed in the animal's rear quarter.

The bull bolted away, but soon began to stagger, then lay down and fell asleep. We put him on the special elk-hauling tarp, loaded him onto a small two-wheeled single-animal trailer pulled by an ATV, and towed him to our large transport trailer. We maneuvered the big guy into the trailer, rolled him over, and removed the tarp.

Bill and a helper were at the front of the elk. Sam and I brought up the rear, dragging the animal into the trailer. Once were able to slide him into the front compartment, we all rested for a bit to try and catch our breath.

The large trailer is divided into two compartments and is made for horses and cows, so the fit is snug for an adult elk and several elk handlers. It can get claustrophobic for people who're inside working on the elk.

Elk are ruminants. They can't lie on their backs with their heads on the ground for very long. That position could kill them because of the way their digestive system works. If they're in a bad position for too long, they could regurgitate stomach contents into their lungs and could develop pneumonia and die. So, while we work on them, we have to hold the elk so it's sitting upright on its *sternum*, or breastbone.

Handling these big, heavy, animals and holding their heads upright is a tough job. The three of us were struggling in the awkward, confined space.

During the transfer process Sam was positioned near the elk's rear quarter where the dart had injected the highly potent drug. While handling the elk, he'd accidentally placed his hand directly on the spot where the dart had hit the animal. Sam was worried he might've gotten an exposure to the tranquilizing drugs. We all knew that it didn't take much to have an adverse effect on a human.

"Hey, Kim," he said. "I feel really weird."

"What's wrong?" I asked.

"I might've touched the place where the dart went in. I think I might've gotten some of the drugs on my hand."

This was a day I'd always dreaded. I asked Sam to sit down, then I tried to think of the quickest way to get him to the hospital. Medical response time would be the key to saving his life. As my mind raced, none of us moved, even the elk. You could've heard a pin drop.

"How do you feel?" I asked.

"My whole body's tingly," he said.

This was not a good situation. I was scared for Sam. If he'd gotten the drug in his system, he might have only a few minutes before he'd go down, and without proper medical help, well, you know what could happen. I tried to act calm, but I was getting a sick feeling.

"Do you have any open cuts on your hands?" I asked.

"No," he said.

"Are you sure?" I asked, and looked at his hands to confirm this for myself.

"Yes," he said, "I'm positive."

"Did you touch your eyes or your nose?"

"No," he said, "But I'm worried some of the drugs might've gotten absorbed through my skin."

I knew the drugs were extremely dangerous if they splashed into your eyes or if you got them in your nose or mouth or into your bloodstream through an open cut or sore. I tried to think back through my years of drug training as quickly as I could, straining to recall whether this particular drug could be absorbed through the skin. I didn't think it could.

I prayed my memory was correct, because Sam's life could depend on it. Sam was getting scared. I was really frightened, too. For lack of any good alternative, I went for the placebo effect and told him in a confident tone, "No, Sam, these drugs can't be absorbed through the skin. There's absolutely no way."

He looked at me and asked in a serious tone, "Are you sure?"

"Yes," I said, "I'm *sure*."

He looked at me for a long moment to make certain my expression matched what I was saying, then he looked back at his hand, gave a big sigh, and said, "Well, I think I'm startin to feel a little better now."

We all let out big sighs of relief. This was no joking matter. From the front of the trailer Bill Stiver spoke up and said he'd experienced the same problem, worrying that he'd gotten some of the drugs on his hand, so he commiserated with Sam. It's an awful feeling, I knew from my own experience.

As if we didn't have enough to worry about, during the time we'd been tending to Sam, the elk had started to wake up. So, we had one problem fixed, but now we had another one to deal with. We needed to get a move on.

It was totally dark inside the trailer now, so we had to use flash-lights to see anything. The elk could hurt itself, or us, if it was al-lowed to wake up inside the trailer slowly, on its own. Because of that I needed to give it the reversal drugs to help it come fully awake quickly.

I got out, grabbed my reversal drugs, and loaded up the syringes. Then I crawled back into the trailer. A 700-pound elk and the three of us, together in the small space, meant there wasn't much room. But I had to administer the reversal drug before the elk roused enough to get violent. The reversal drugs are Naltrexone and Yohimbine. We give half the drugs under the skin, subcutaneously, and half of them into a vein, intravenously.

Normally I would give the injection under the skin first, because the intravenous shot takes effect a lot more quickly than the subcutaneous shot. That meant that once I've given the IV drugs, I need to get out of the way *fast*. But this time I didn't do it that way. There wasn't much light or room so I decided I should first try to get the difficult part of the job out of the way, penetrating the elk's thick hair and skin with a needle and finding a vein.

The animal was very heavy and sluggish. I gave it the IV medicine and could see the elk raising his head. "We better hurry!" I said. Then, when I stuck the second injection under the skin, the elk started trying to stand up. I struggled to hold it down until I was finished, shouting to the others, "Get outta the truck!"

Sam and Bill clambered out and closed the door behind them so the elk couldn't escape. I didn't dare leave, though, until I'd emptied the second syringe into the elk. I held the bull's large antlers. He was kicking and thrashing, trying to get up. I warned my helpers to be ready to open the trailer door fast when I finished the second injection.

The plunger hit bottom and I pulled the syringe out, shouting, "Open the door!"

They did, and I leaped out and Bill and Sam slammed and latched the door. The bull was up and giving us dirty looks from inside his prison. The three of us stood there, breathless, listening to the angry elk clanking his antlers back and forth inside the trailer.

That had been a close call, for all of us. We were lucky and everything turned out okay, but episodes like this were causing more and more gray hairs to appear.

YOU SHOT WHAT?

IT TAKES EXPERIENCE, skill, and a little luck to safely capture free ranging wild animals with a dart gun. There's a lot more involved than just mechanical procedures. There are emotional and psychological issues you have to cope with, too.

You have to learn to use the tools, like a dart rifle and pistol, and you have to learn how to calculate the dosages of the drugs and load the darts. It's stressful, especially when you're preparing to dart a big animal that can turn on you and do serious damage. If you miscalculate the dose, either nothing will happen or the animal could die. It's especially tough when you're handling a chemical that can be deadly to both humans and animals. An error in judgment can result in horrible consequences.

It can be difficult even when you're shooting practice darts at a stationary target, as I found out when I was instructing Jennifer Murrow, an elk researcher from the University of Tennessee.

Jennifer and I had a special relationship. It was more like a parent with a rebellious, vocal teenager, than a boss with a young employee. Sometimes she treated me like a father figure, and other times like an annoying big brother.

We'd spent more than one long, boring evening together sitting in the Ford Explorer on elk stakeouts. We'd wait for an elk to show up so we could capture it and replace its radio collar or move it back to the Park if it had wandered into a *No Elk Zone,* an area with a lot of farming activity. During the many dull hours of waiting for a specific elk to walk by, we talked.

On one of the long waits, we'd talked about nearly everything either of us could think of when I said, "Okay, you tell me what you don't like about me and I'll tell you what I don't like about you."

She was very quick to tell me what she didn't like about me. She complained that I was too controlling and wouldn't allow anyone else to dart an elk.

Jennifer was technically not a government employee and didn't have the official training, so she wasn't permitted to shoot the dart gun or dart an elk. I wasn't supposed to allow her do any of these things, but when she wanted something, she could be *extremely* persistent.

She bugged the fool out of me to let her dart an elk. I knew Jennifer had a long career ahead of her working with wildlife, and that she needed to develop shooting skills. So, eventually her persistence won out. I gave in and told her I'd train her to dart elk, *someday*.

There's an art to successful wildlife capture using darts, guns, and drugs. You're trying to shoot a big dart into a live wild animal that might be fifteen or even fifty yards away. The skill is similar to that of archery or bow-hunting. You need to have the right equipment, but you also have to know how to use it, and understand its limitations.

Once you've mastered the ability to make the dart go precisely where you want it to go, you have to be able to approach a wild animal on *its* terms and in *its* home. Many people fall short in this skill of stalking.

In addition to being proficient with your dart gun, you have to have enough skills as a woodsman to be able to get close to the animal without spooking it. The person responsible for pulling the trigger has to be able to put a lot of skills together to safely capture a large wild animal without harming the critter, any bystanders, or themselves.

Capturing elk, or any animal, with a dart gun depends on both little and big things. You need to be able to adjust one thing, or ten things, at the snap of a finger. If you mess up on any single aspect of the process, either the show is over, or an animal or person could be seriously hurt, or worse.

A long list of things runs through my head before I shoot. Things like:

- How much does the elk weigh?
- Am I using the right drug combination?
- Am I using the right dosages?
- Am I using the correct setting on my dart gun?
- Did I spill any of the Carfentanil on my hand?
- Do I have the correct explosive charge to propel the dart?
- Which way is the wind blowing?
- Can I hold the dart gun steady enough to make a good shot?
- Is my angle toward the elk good?
- Can I hit the elk in the hip?
- Am I too close or too far away from the elk?
- Could the elk fall into a creek or run off a cliff after I dart it?
- Are the spectators observing from a safe location?

I hoped that Jennifer and others could understand my reluctance to hand over a rifle and bottles filled with dangerous drugs, and assume things would go well. A simple mishap or error in judgment could not only result in a dead elk, but also in the loss of someone's life, including my own.

Jennifer and I talked about how to calculate the right dosage of the drugs, how to decide which dart to use, when to use the various different sizes of explosive charges on the cartridge, and many other things. Jennifer was very smart, actually much smarter than me, but the one thing I had on my side was experience. Experience was important.

We typically used a .22 blank charge to propel the dart, but you still had to decide what power setting to use on the dart gun. There are four settings that range from twenty to fifty yards, and you have to take into account distance, and the general direction and speed of the wind. There's a lot to consider.

To make matters worse, we're often working in front of a crowd, so not only do you have to be very good at evaluating the position of the animal, but also you have to be extremely aware of the movements of all the people around you. There are many moving targets.

Many people wanted to shoot the gun. But Jennifer kept bugging me until I finally agreed to let her try to dart an elk. I intended to pick one I knew would allow us to get fairly close without freaking out and running away.

We went through the verbal training. We practiced the entire procedure from loading the dart to taking the shot. Then we set up a stationary target about thirty yards away. Jennifer leaned against the hood of my truck and lined up her first practice shot with a practice dart. A practice dart isn't loaded with actual drugs, but instead is weighted to shoot just like a dart with drugs in it.

Jennifer was taking a long time fiddling with the gun, trying to get ready to shoot. I told her I needed to go to the bathroom and said I'd be back soon. I really just wanted to get away so I wouldn't be watching her during her first try because I knew that would put additional pressure on her.

As I walked a few yards away from the vehicle, I heard the dart rifle go off and then I heard an awful metallic sound, so I hurried back to see what had made the noise. "What the heck happened?" I asked.

"I don't know," she said, with her eyebrows deeply furrowed. "I just aimed the gun and shot. But when I pulled the trigger I heard this weird sound!"

"Where'd the dart go?" I asked.

"I have no idea," Jennifer said, "I didn't see where it went."

I took the gun from her and lined up where it had been pointed and I found the dart stuck in a tree about ten feet above the target. I asked Jennifer if she'd put the crosshairs on the center of the target. She said she had.

Then what made the dart shoot so high? I wondered.

As we both stood in silence, looking around, trying to understand what had happened, I glanced toward where Jennifer was leaning on the truck. I noticed there was a long scar on the hood that hadn't been there before. When I looked closer, I could see a four-inch scratch across the front of my truck.

"You shot my truck!" I shouted.

"I'm sorry," she said. "I didn't mean to. I'll pay for it."

"Do you know how much paperwork I'll have to do now?" I complained.

She looked at me like a whipped puppy. I knew it was an accident and started to feel sorry for her and ashamed for shouting at her. I apologized for yelling. Then I looked at the crease in the hood again, and said, "Well, it's actually not that bad. Maybe we can fix it ourselves and not have to do any paperwork," although I really didn't believe that.

I suggested we think of it as *just a flesh wound*. I thought, but didn't say, *at least she didn't shoot* me!

Jennifer was ashamed and embarrassed, as you'd expect, and she apologized profusely. But, of course, these things happen. That's why we practice.

I told myself the damage to the truck looked sort of like hail damage. It actually looked more like where a farmer had plowed a furrow of ground. It looked especially bad if you were standing at just the right angle with good light. I repaired it myself as best I could using the little bottle of white touchup paint that came with the vehicle. It was old and didn't match exactly, but it helped conceal the bullet wound well enough that neither of us got into trouble over it.

The rest of the day, Jennifer kept looking at me without saying anything. I knew what she was thinking, though, so every so often I'd look at her and say, "Jennifer, it happens."

FLIRTING WITH DISASTER

IT WAS NIGHT IN OCONALUFTEE, North Carolina, on the Cherokee Tribal Land—which meant it was full dark. There was no light in the valley except for the moon and stars.

I was down on my knees on the ground holding Elk Cow #5, waiting for the reversal drug to take effect. It had been a challenge to capture this elk because she'd been darted a few times before. She knew what we were up to whenever we approached her.

Now that I had the elk in hand again, I wanted to be sure we did her no harm. That meant I didn't want to let her go until she was good and awake because there was a river close by, just through the line of trees that bordered the meadow where she lay.

I was worried she might run right toward the river in an effort to reach the cover of the trees, and I didn't want her to stagger off into the water by accident and get hurt or maybe even drown because she was woozy from the drugs I'd darted her with.

I had a few helpers with me that night. Jennifer Murrow, the Ph.D. student, was there. Steven Dobey, a Park wildlife biologist who worked mainly on our elk project in North Carolina, was helping, too.

We also had Joyce Cooper, a Rocky Mountain Elk Foundation volunteer who worked tirelessly to help raise money for our elk project. Joyce and many other Elk Foundation volunteers had whole-heartedly supported our elk project from the beginning. Without help from Joyce and the other volunteers, I don't think we'd have elk in the Park today.

After we completed our work on the elk, I asked my helpers to move all the equipment back and make plenty of room for the elk to jump up and run away.

They moved most of the gear a safe distance away, but Steven and

Jennifer remained nearby. Steven was holding a handful of needles and Jennifer had the drug kit. Steven was wearing a headlamp with the light turned on. A light isn't a good idea if you want to keep a wild animal calm, especially at night when the animal has been captured and poked and prodded and is waking up from a deep sleep. I could hear Steven talking, too.

"Be quiet," I whispered, "and turn that headlamp off."

He apparently didn't hear me, so I said it again, a little louder.

"Be quiet and turn your light off."

Apparently Steven was a little more interested in Jennifer than he was in me or the elk, so I said it for a third time even louder. But his headlamp continued to shine in my direction.

By now the elk was partially awake and struggling to get up. I couldn't hold her much longer and I'd lost my patience, so I hollered, "Turn off that light!"

Of course that was stupid on my part. When I shouted, it was the last straw for the elk cow. She leaped up and charged straight toward the light. Steven and Jennifer took off, racing across the field just ahead of the elk, with Steven carrying a handful of needles.

I was left lying on the ground in the dark, alone. All I could see was the light of the headlamp dancing around crazily, pointing every which way as Steven ran.

When I caught up with the group, I asked if everyone was okay. They were all fine, although Steven said that when Elk #5 was charging toward him, his life flashed before his eyes. He and Jennifer were lucky they didn't get seriously injured. Looking on the bright side, at least the elk had run away from the river.

When we were all standing safely beside the truck, Steven finally turned his headlamp off. I looked at him, and said, "It's okay to have your headlamp on *now*."

I'm not sure if this episode had anything to do with it or not, but Steven and Jennifer ended up getting married.

DOWNTOWN ELK

THEY'RE CALLED WILDLIFE for a reason. It's tough to keep up with wild animals, especially in the mountains. Tracking elk on the ground can be impossible at times, even with the aid of radio-telemetry equipment. Because of the rough topography and the time it takes to hike into remote areas, sometimes we needed to use an airplane to locate them.

We mount a receiver antenna on the wing of the airplane. Then, once a signal is located, the pilot circles in a tight pattern until we can pinpoint the exact location of the elk on the ground.

One day when Steven Dobey was flying near Waynesville, North Carolina, attempting to locate each of the elk, he detected a signal from an animal collar coming from an unexpected direction. The pilot flew around until he'd homed in on it. The signal was coming from Sevierville, Tennessee, which was over forty miles away as the crow flies. That wasn't a place where an elk or an elk collar should be.

Steven and the pilot agreed that they needed to fly closer to be sure. They pinpointed the signal. It was coming from a house in a subdivision in the middle of the City of Sevierville. Once Steven was on the ground, he called me and told me what he'd found. Obviously, my first thought was that someone had poached an elk; and that the collar and the meat were inside their house. Apparently they were unaware that we could track the collar.

I called the local wildlife officer, David Sexton, and told him what was going on. He said he'd meet us in Sevierville and Steven could point out which house the radio signal was coming from. When everyone was assembled, it was easy to confirm that the signal was indeed coming from inside a specific house on a particular street. We thought we'd caught a poacher and that an arrest was imminent.

We went to a nearby lot with a good vantage point. We saw a car drive up to the house. It pulled into the driveway and a lady got out and walked back to the mailbox.

"That lady looks familiar," I said, "I think I know her."

I watched the lady through my binoculars. "That's Lois!" I said. "She's married to Chuck Hester. He works for the wildlife department as a hog hunter."

As the words left my mouth, I started to put two and two together as to why an elk collar would be in his house. I started to laugh under my breath. I turned to the others, and said, "No poacher lives here."

I had an idea why there was a signal coming from the house, so we drove over to have a chat with Lois. After a brief howdy, I told her Steven had picked up a signal from a transmitter coming from inside their house that was broadcasting all the way to Waynesville, North Carolina.

She invited us to come in and take a look. Steven turned on his telemetry receiver. We could hear a loud *beep-beep-beep-beep*. We tracked the signal into the garage and to a footlocker.

It was the locker where Chuck kept his Park backpack. Lois opened it. We rummaged through Chuck's backpack and found the source of the signal down at the bottom, a transmitter we'd removed from an old radio-tracking collar.

Every member of the wildlife crew had to travel in the backcountry to hunt hogs, investigate bear problems, or conduct animal surveys. Because of the potential danger of hiking and camping alone in the backcountry, I wanted a way to locate each person if for any reason they became unable to radio for help.

We had some old radio-telemetry collars left over from early bear and wild hog research projects, so I'd asked each member of the crew to carry one of the collars whenever they were in the backcountry. Then, if they got into trouble, we could locate them in the same way we'd found Chuck's transmitter—even when it was inside a backpack, a locker, a garage, and a house, in the middle of Sevierville.

The transmitter at Chuck's house was still switched on because the devices didn't have an *on/off* switch. To stop the signal, a magnet has to be placed on the transmitter. To start it again, you simply removed the magnet.

Each of the transmitters operates on a unique frequency. The frequency of Chuck's transmitter and the frequency of the transmitter on the elk we were looking for were so close, Steven had picked up both signals. After the embarrassing *poacher* fiasco we made a policy change. Anyone who left the Park was asked to tape a magnet to their transmitter.

We were able to find the lost elk the next day. He was fine. This was another lesson learned about technology and wildlife management. There's wisdom in the old saying, *Things are not always as they appear.*

UP A CREEK

THE GUYS WHO DO HOG CONTROL in the Smokies are a unique breed. They have to be because their job is demanding and dangerous. Backcountry hog control is a physically challenging job because you work cross-country in rough terrain. It's also mentally challenging because you're trying to outwit one of the most intelligent creatures on the face of the earth, wild hogs. And often you have to be able to work alone.

The lack of nearby backup from another ranger exacerbates the danger. There's a significant risk of slipping, falling, getting bitten by a snake, stung by yellow jackets, or attacked by bears or hogs. There's no telling what will happen when you're out alone in a mountainous wilderness exposed to a wide range of unpredictable weather conditions.

To reach to the remote stretches of the backcountry, hog hunters sometimes have to travel long distances—using a four-wheel drive vehicle to get to the trailhead, then proceeding on foot to the area where they will be working. It's very important to keep track of who's going where, and when. The hunters call Park Dispatch to let them know which camp they'll be using and what area they'll be working in for the week.

They call Dispatch again when they leave camp or travel off-trail, to give more specifics about the route they plan to use, with estimated beginning and ending times. Then they call when they're back at camp for the night. When they leave, they call Dispatch and let them know they're out of the backcountry. If something goes wrong, they might call in earlier.

One of the best hog hunters, Dale Raxter, got into an extremely dangerous situation once when he was working off-trail in the middle of winter in Hazel Creek, North Carolina. Much of the Hazel Creek drainage area is remote and inaccessible. Dale wanted to travel cross-country to look for wild hogs in uncharted areas. He knew it would be rough going and risky, but he's a tough, competent guy who knows how to handle himself in the mountains.

If a Jeep was needed at Hazel Creek, the wildlife department had to haul one across Fontana Lake by using our maintenance division's barge, because there's no road access to the creek. When necessary, we kept a vehicle over there for use on wildlife projects. On this trip, Dale used the Jeep to drive along a backcountry road up through the Hazel Creek drainage to the area where he wanted to work, and from there he set out on foot.

After he left the safety of the vehicle, he crossed the boisterous creek that gives the area its name, and continued traveling, making his way northeast, climbing in elevation toward the crest of the ridge, looking for wild hogs. Before he left, he'd radioed Dispatch and explained roughly where he planned to go. But when you're hog hunting in an area you've never been in before, you don't know exactly where you're going, so therein lies the risk.

Dale had been working the cross-country area for most of the morning. At about 2 o'clock in the afternoon, he called *700*, Park Dispatch, to alert them that he was on foot, off-trail in the Hazel Creek drainage area, and wasn't sure exactly where he was, or if he'd be able to make it back to his vehicle by dark.

In January, with the temperatures going down with the sun, this was a serious concern, especially because Dale had to cross Hazel Creek on his way back. Like many of the cold, fast-running streams in the Smokies, during wet weather they can become the size of a river in some places. No one would last long out in the wilderness alone if they got soaking wet when the temperatures went well below freezing.

Dale had unexpectedly gotten into a huge boulder field. There were enormous crevices between the rocks. He had to jump from the top of one boulder to another to make his way across. He knew we'd never find him if he fell into one of the crevices and he feared he might not be able to extricate himself.

Dale had to be pretty concerned to call us, but thank goodness he was smart enough to do it. From his voice on the radio, you could hear his anxiety. Normally our guys don't ask for help. So, when they do, we know they've exhausted all other options.

The first problem was that Dale wasn't exactly sure where he was. He was across Hazel Creek on the side of a mountain in the middle of a giant boulder field, but he didn't know how far away he was from the creek, or from his vehicle. In those days, GPSs were not available like they are today. Dale had been sweating heavily from the exertion of traversing the boulders and he'd soaked his clothes. When he slowed down, he knew he'd get cold, so he had to keep moving.

"If I get wet in the creek and there's no one to pick me up," he told Dispatch, "I could be in serious trouble."

Everyone in the Park was listening attentively to the radio conversation. As soon as the North Carolina rangers heard Dale's call for help, several of them dropped what they were doing and headed to Fontana Boat Dock to pick up a boat and travel to Hazel Creek. Field staff throughout the Park help each other, but the North Carolina rangers really stick together because of the remoteness of their work area and the associated dangers.

Although Dale worked in a different division, he was still one of their own and we knew they'd do everything in their power to help him. The rangers crossed Fontana Lake, then made a six-mile drive up the creek to the area where they thought Dale might come out.

All this time, Dale continued trying to work his way back, side-hilling, not sure when he might find the road or where exactly he might come out, if he was able to get out at all. The rangers' rescue plan was to drive along the road looking for Dale's vehicle. Then, when they found it, they'd try to locate him starting from there.

The North Carolina rangers found Dale's Jeep and started searching along the creek. Dale was able to talk to them on Channel 1 of the Park radio. This was good news because Channel 1 isn't on a repeater. When the rangers use Channel 1, their radios are functioning like walkie-talkies. So, they knew they had to be relatively close to each other, possibly within a mile or so.

Dale still didn't know exactly where he was, but he reported that he'd made it to what he thought was Hazel Creek. The creek was running high and he was going to have to get wet to get across. It was dark now and the rangers couldn't see him, so Dale asked them to switch the Jeep's headlights on. They did and they continued driving along the road on the other side of the creek. Dale scanned the forest until he was finally able see them.

"I see your lights!" he said.

He asked them to continue down the road about 200 yards and then stop. He searched for a place to ford the creek as close to the lights as he could manage and the rangers picked him up when he got to the other side. They'd helped orient him out of the wilderness and now they transported him back to safety. Disaster had been averted.

Dale's a real mountain man from North Carolina. But for even the most experienced person, the Park is dangerous and not very forgiving, at night, in winter, and especially going cross-country, off-trail in a boulder field.

After this incident I knew we had to do something to make it safer for our guys when they were out in the field, so we improvised a solution. That's when we started carrying radio transmitters left over from collars we'd used on bears and wild hogs in previous research projects. Each collar broadcasted on a distinctive frequency, so we could always track them and pinpoint their location if anyone got hurt, or trapped, or become unconscious. It wasn't a foolproof system, but it made us all feel a little safer.

The wildlife crew was the first bunch in the Park to use personal locators this way.

The first thing every morning, we'd check with Dispatch to confirm that everyone had made contact. If anyone had failed to check in, we'd give them a call. If there was no answer, then someone would immediately hit the trail and hike to the missing person's camp to see if they were okay.

Although nearly every time we had to send someone up the mountain to look for a hunter who hadn't checked out the previous night, it turned out to be because of a faulty radio or dead batteries, it was always worth it, just in case.

BAD BEAR DAY

THE MOST BIZZARE DAY I ever experienced with regard to wildlife management was when we had three scary encounters between people and bears, in different areas of the Park, all on the same day.

The day started off wrong early in the morning with a report from a backpacker that a bear had been trying to break into the Mt. Collins Shelter while there were campers inside. The Mount Collins Shelter is along the Appalachian Trail between Clingmans Dome and Newfound Gap. The Appalachian Trail parallels Clingmans Dome Road for about eight miles; and there's a short connecting trail from the Dome road over to the shelter. This means the shelter is very accessible, so it's heavily used by campers.

For years we'd had problems up there with nuisance bears. There'd been several different incidents with bears trying to get food from people at the shelter. One bear made frequent visits to a nearby parking lot used by backpackers who wanted to leave their cars at the trailhead while they camped in the backcountry. He bit a car tire and deflated it.

He also bit a car's back bumper and chewed up both windshield wipers. In addition to traditional food items, bears are sometimes attracted to leather, vinyl, and plastic. We've had bears tear the seat off our Polaris Ranger Utility Vehicle. They've also damaged vinyl swimming pool and hot tub covers in Gatlinburg.

So when we got an early morning call from Dispatch saying some campers were having trouble with a bear at Mt. Collins Shelter, I sent someone to see what the situation was. When he arrived, the ranger was told about the incident. Back then, the shelters were made with rock walls on the sides and back and chain link fencing on the front. The roof was made of tin sheeting.

Sometime after midnight, the people camping inside the shelter heard a bear walking on the roof. Then, suddenly, the bear ripped the roof open, and reached down into the shelter. There were seven people camping inside. The place erupted into chaos as the campers fought with the bear.

They screamed and yelled and flailed at it with their hiking sticks. Adrenaline has a way of energizing people who fear for their lives. After a lengthy battle, the campers were successful in fighting the bear off and forcing it to leave the immediate area of the shelter.

At dawn the bear returned. The campers, as a group, went on the attack again, and were able to run the bear off again. Then they hiked out together until they located a maintenance person at Newfound Gap who radioed the incident to Dispatch who then relayed the hikers' call for help to us.

Dispatch called me on the phone and asked me to listen to the hikers talking over the radio. Once I heard what was going on, I told the maintenance employee to ask the campers to stop by Headquarters on their way home to let me know the details of the encounter.

This was a serious problem that we'd have to do something about, sooner rather than later. A bear that's bold enough to rip the roof off a shelter and fight with the campers inside is a very dangerous bear. We were lucky that time, but who knew what might happen to the next hiker coming down the trail to camp at Mt. Collins.

The group reported that one of the ladies was menstruating and, back in those days, the thinking was that this would attract a bear. Although many researchers have tried to correlate bear aggression with women's monthly cycles, no research has ever proven this to be a valid issue.

Later in the day, we closed the shelter to give us time to introduce this bear to our Smokies bear management crew. If the bear was smart, he'd look for another place to eat.

A few hours later, in the afternoon, a law enforcement ranger, Jamie Sanders, was hiking from Cades Cove to Russell Field Shelter to post bear warning signs. We'd received a report of a bear harassing campers there, too. All of the wildlife crew was out working on various bear-related problems in different areas of the Park, so we'd asked the Cades Cove Rangers if they had anyone who'd hike up to post the warning signs. Jamie agreed to go.

When Jamie was a short distance above Backcountry Campsite #10, Ledbetter Ridge, on Russell Field Trail, she heard something loud running through the brush uphill from her, closing in on her location fast. Then suddenly an adult bear popped out on the trail about fifty yards ahead of her.

The bear took one look at her and immediately ran toward her in a full charge. If you've never been in this situation, I can tell you, it's one of the scariest moments in your life. I've been there, I know. You don't have time to think about what you should do, you just respond the best you can.

As the bear came closer and closer, Jamie shouted, "Hey, bear!"

But it didn't stop.

When the bear charged to within five yards of her, Jamie retreated and fired one shot from her 40mm service revolver. Her intention was to shoot the charging animal, but she thought the shot had probably missed. The loud noise of the firearm discharging at very close range, however, stopped its charge. That had been Jamie's primary motive in shooting anyway, to stop the bear's charge. Fortunately, it worked.

Although the bear was no longer coming any closer to Jamie, it began vocalizing by making growling, huffing, and grunting sounds. The bear was extremely upset and, at one point, swatted the ground hard, throwing rocks and dirt toward her. Jamie observed the bear and was fairly certain she hadn't injured it in any way. She had no idea why it had charged her, or why it was now making strange noises. She'd done nothing to provoke the animal.

The bear continued to make growling and huffing sounds, but didn't leave the area. If the bear had been hit with a bullet, it would've continued with its attack, run off, or died. But for the bear to turn around and slowly walk away growling in a low tone and popping its jaws was very odd.

These bear vocalizations seemed to be indications of *defensive* behavior toward Jamie. It was something a mother bear would do if she was trying to defend herself, her cub, her territory, or her food. But why had the bear aggressively charged Jamie in the first place?

In some cases, a charge similar to this could be interpreted as an *offensive* behavior. An aggressive charge made you think the bear was trying to get human food, or maybe considering Jamie herself as prey and a potential source of food.

The bear finally went back up the trail a short distance, but remained nearby. Jamie wondered why it wouldn't leave. It was strange. She stayed in the area, too, just in case she might've hit the bear, and called for assistance.

Andrew Herrington, who'd started his career with us in the wildlife department and was now working as a law enforcement ranger, responded to help.

As Andrew approached the site of the mysterious attack where Jamie was waiting, he saw a huge male bear walking away on the lower side of the trail. He assumed this was the same bear that had charged Jamie, but later we realized this wasn't the case at all.

When Andrew joined up with Jamie they heard a noise and looked up the trail. Jamie hadn't realized it, but just below her was a small cub high up in a tree watching the whole incident unfold. Something was sliding down a tree when they looked up they saw a furry black cub rapidly descending.

By now, the mother bear had moved off the trail to a place where the cub could see her. Rather than safely sliding down the tree to the ground, Jamie said the cub unexpectedly jumped out of the tree from high up, then hit the ground, and ran to join its mom. They saw the mother bear with her small cub hastily move up the trail away from them and out of sight.

In hindsight, we think the adult bear that charged Jamie was a mother bear who was separated from her cub. After the confrontation with Jamie, the mother bear lingered in the area until she was able to hook up with her cub, and then she left with it.

I asked Andrew about wind direction. At the time of the attack there was a crosswind. So there was little chance that the bear charging down the hill could've smelled Jamie hiking up the trail. The mother bear had to be charging down the hill for some other reason.

Jamie had heard the bear running through the brush, coming from a fairly long distance, so the bear had probably not realized Jamie was there.

After evaluating the incident, we concluded that the mother bear and cub were separated while the mother was browsing for food. The mother was on the uphill side of the trail and her cub was in a tree on the downhill side of the trail. It's normal for mother bears to put their cubs up in a tree for safety while she looks for food. If the cub stayed on the ground with mom while she was busy feeding, another bear could possibly grab it and kill it. So, a cub that's safely hanging out in the top of a tree is a much better strategy for both the mom and the cub.

Apparently a large male bear showed up in the area, downhill from the cub. Male bears are naturally programmed to kill every cub they find in an effort to maintain dominance in their territory. The male bear was probably the one Andrew Herrington saw leaving the area as he arrived. If the big male bear got close enough to the cub, it would kill it. If the cub felt threatened, it would cry for help. The momma bear must've heard her cub's cry for help and was charging to rescue it.

The mother bear probably didn't know exactly what the threat to her cub was, but it didn't matter to her. She was in overdrive, running down the hill, coming to save it. Jamie, hiking along the trail, minding her own business, just happened to be at the wrong place at the wrong time. The bear saw her and assumed she was the problem.

This, I believe, was the reason the bear charged her. The loud report from Jamie's pistol stopped the charge and scared the mother bear, but she wouldn't leave the area until she found her cub.

Later, there might've been a confrontation between the mother bear and the big male bear. If so, the mother bear probably ran the male bear off.

After the mother and cub left the area, Andrew left and Jamie was able to continue her hike to the shelter and post the warning signs for other hikers.

Jamie did all the things necessary to protect herself. If it had been a Park visitor instead of Jamie, they might've made mistakes like trying to run away or play dead. We'll never know what would've happened then.

All in all, things ended up about as well as anyone could've hoped for. Jamie wasn't injured and none of the bears were hurt either.

🐾　🐾　🐾　🐾　🐾

Information about these encounters was being relayed to me on the radio so the word about the bear incidents was spreading. It was late afternoon when Park Superintendent, Dale Ditmanson, came by for an update on the bear problems. While the Superintendent was standing in the doorway of my office, the campers arrived from the Mt. Collins Shelter to give us the details about the bear trying to break in through the roof. The Superintendent wanted to hear what they had to say, so he pulled up a chair, and listened.

While I was debriefing the frightened campers, the phone rang again. I couldn't believe it. It was Dispatch saying they had the Blount County Sheriff's Department on the phone. The Sheriff was reporting that earlier in the afternoon, Scott Higdon, a man from Florida, had been attacked by a bear on Little River Road. It was a very disturbing incident, a potential brush with death. Higdon had been seriously injured.

We were told Higdon was on his way to Blount Memorial Hospital.

Ranger Steve Cooper went to the hospital to check on Higdon and find out what had happened. Both of Higdon's legs from the knees down were extremely dirty and his arms were covered with dirt, too. His shorts, shoes, and socks were bloody. Many of Higdon's wounds were still actively oozing blood. There were three holes in the top of his right shoe that matched three puncture wounds on the top of his right foot.

Higdon said he was driving on Little River Road past the Sinks toward Townsend. The Sinks is a scenic area filled with dangerous rapids and deeps pools. Many naïve visitors have died there when, despite all the posted warnings, they attempt to ride an inner tube over the falls and drown or dive off the cliffs and break their necks in the shallow, rocky stream.

As he drove around a curve, Higdon said he saw a bear dart across the road and disappear down a steep rocky bank, heading toward the river. He pulled off the road, hoping to photograph it.

He said he jumped out of his car and ran to the side of the road and looked over the edge of the bank, but was startled when he realized the bear was crouched down just below where he was standing. The bear was frightened by the sudden appearance of Higdon looming over it. It charged up the bank and attacked him.

Higdon said he tripped when he tried to back up. The bear lunged at him and grabbed his right leg, at which point he fell down the bank and landed on top of the bear. He grabbed at a sapling to keep from sliding any further, but by then he was already eye-to-eye with the angry bear.

The bear bit and scratched its way up Higdon's legs. The animal bit him several times on the ankles, lower legs, and the inside of his thighs. Higdon said he guessed the bear weighed about 150 pounds and he believed it was a male.

If the bear had continued to bite and claw the flesh any farther up his legs, Higdon could've landed a part as a high tenor in a church choir, if he'd managed to stay alive. Higdon said he struck the bear a couple of times with his walking stick. He said he kicked and fought and screamed and finally got the bear to release his right foot but then it bit his left foot. He kicked at the bear and poked the animal in the eye with his stick. Then it released him, and turned and ran down the bank toward the river.

Higdon's wounds were bad. He had lacerations, scratches, and puncture wounds on both legs and feet. After treatment on Friday, he was released from the hospital. Ranger Cooper and another ranger planned to continue the interview the following Monday. When they arrived where he was staying on Monday morning, Higdon was sitting in a wheelchair with bandages on both feet. He told the rangers that he'd been at Elkmont on Friday working on his grand-parents' graves. The graves had sunk and he'd been leveling the plots with more dirt.

He said he left the cemetery around 8:30 p.m. After the second interview the rangers told Higdon they wanted to meet with him in the morning and travel to the site where the attack occurred. It was important for us to know exactly where it happened so we could warn other visitors.

The next morning the rangers went back to meet Higdon, but he was gone. They talked to a neighbor and were told that he'd gone back home to Florida early that morning.

There remained an element of mystery and confusion about this third bear attack that we were never able to fully resolve. It was certainly a strange ordeal. Why did Higdon leave early and stand the rangers up for the scheduled meeting? What was he hiding? Clearly he'd been in a struggle with something that had big teeth.

It was just odd. The whole day was odd. The bear trying to tear into the Mt. Collins Shelter, the Cades Cove ranger having to shoot to stop a charging bear, and now a Florida man unexpectedly at-tacked by a bear on the side of a road. What a strange day.

It was one of those days that you're just happy when it's over. It was a bad bear day.

THE TROUBLE WITH ANTLERS

IT WAS ON A FRIDAY AFTERNOON near quitting time when I got the call. I was gathering my things to leave Park Headquarters when Dispatch relayed a report about a deer caught in a food storage cable system at Backcountry Campsite #28, Marks Cove.

I asked Dispatch to see if anyone was scheduled to be camping at Marks Cove that night. They checked, and said there were no reservations. That meant it was important for someone to go up there. Left to struggle overnight, there was a good chance the deer would die of exhaustion and stress, or choke to death, or be killed by a bear.

All the hog hunters had already gone home tired, hungry, dirty, and sleep-deprived after a long week in the backcountry searching for wild pigs. I was sure they were all looking forward to the weekend and that going back to work wasn't on anyone's list of things they wanted to do.

Ranger Dan Nolfi lived in Park housing just behind Headquarters, so I gave him a call to see if he was available, and willing to hike up to Marks Cove to verify the report of the tangled deer and release it, if it was still there.

Dan was willing, although not excited, to drive twenty-five miles, then hike nearly six miles uphill to check on the deer. Dan was one of the men that I was very happy to have on our team. He'd always do whatever was necessary to help out and I really appreciated him for that. Dan was as comfortable in the backcountry as other people would be in their home. He was a modern day mountain man.

When Dan arrived at Marks Cove it was getting dark. Sure enough, an eight-point buck was there and tangled up in a mess of strong aircraft cable that Rick Varner and crew had installed years earlier. It wasn't going to be able to escape on its own. It needed help. Its antlers were snagged and it was going berserk trying to get loose.

It's quite a challenge to deal with an animal the size of full-grown buck, especially one that was fighting for its life. If the deer realized Dan was there to help him, things might've been easier, but it didn't. In the deer's mind, Dan was a serious danger, so he responded accordingly. He twisted and turned and flipped every which way.

With the formidable weapons nature had given him, four sharp pointed hooves and eight dagger-like points on the rack perched on top of his head, the buck could inflict severe injury or even kill other living creatures. Dan hoped he wouldn't be one of them.

At first Dan tried to free the deer by physically manhandling it. He wrestled with the buck, shoving it this way and that, jumping back and forth to keep from being gored as he gradually worked the cable loose. But the deer got more and more upset. It began to bellow for help. This added a new dimension of danger.

Dan was worried that the deer's loud vocalizing might call in a hungry bear looking for an easy meal. When a bear responds to a deer in distress, it doesn't enter the scene casually. It charges in with the intention of killing something. It was dark by this time and Dan's ability to keep an eye on his surroundings was very limited. Finally, he threw in the towel and decided to use immobilization drugs to calm the deer down so he could release it.

Dan injected the deer using a pole syringe, and it soon started to relax. He had to cut the food storage cable in several places, but then he was able to unravel the bird's nest of wire entangling the deer's antlers and free the tired, frazzled, and drugged creature.

Dan was sweating and shaking with adrenalin and exhaustion, but he rested and got his breath back as he sat with the deer for an hour waiting for the drugs to wear off. Eventually the deer stood up and slowly walked away. Before it vanished into the forest, Dan said it stopped for a moment and turned to look back at him.

Of course, we can never know for sure what a deer is thinking but, in this case, I guess it might've been, *Thank you, Dan. I owe you one.*

Dan gathered up all his equipment and hiked six miles in the dark back to his vehicle, then drove to Headquarters and put his gear away. Now, finally, he was ready for a much needed weekend.

So was the deer.

Elk #81 was a rambling bull from Cataloochee. For several years, he left his home repeatedly to travel over the mountain to Tennessee. Usually, he'd take off sometime between Thanksgiving and Christmas. By air, it's about twenty miles, but it's probably twice that distance when you're walking up and down the mountains.

We're not sure why Elk #81 left the main herd in Cataloochee each fall. Maybe he was looking for new friends. Maybe he was kicked out by the other elk. Maybe he was looking for females or for better food. Whatever the reason, he was nicknamed *Rambler* by the locals in honor of his frequent travels.

About twice a week, the elk crew used their radio receivers to locate each of the elk that were wearing radio collars. That's the way we kept track of the herd. Normally, most of the elk could be located in the Cataloochee area, around the town of Cherokee, up in the higher elevations along the Blue Ridge Parkway, or along the Balsam Mountain Spur Road that separated the Park from the Cherokee Tribal Lands.

One December I got a call from Steven Dobey. He'd been tracking the herd and was frustrated because he couldn't locate Elk #81, the Rambler. He said he'd searched in all the normal range in North

Carolina, but couldn't find a signal from him. He wanted to schedule a flight so he could check a wider area. When tracking from an airplane, there aren't as many obstacles to block the signal, so you could usually find the animal, or at least its collar.

Steven drove to Morristown, Tennessee to meet the pilot.

Once they were in the air, it didn't take long to locate the signal from the Rambler. Steven called Dispatch to let them know he was returning to the airport. Then he called me and said he'd found the Rambler in the Baxter Orchard area, along Hwy. 321 between Gatlinburg and Cosby, Tennessee.

I asked him to drive over and check out the situation and try to see why the elk was hanging out in Baxter Orchard. Steven found Rambler near a house. After talking with several locals, he learned that a lady had been feeding apples to Rambler in her backyard. Apparently people were encouraged to buy apples from the Orchard to feed him with.

This wasn't a good situation. It's legal to feed wildlife, including elk, but it's not wise for the safety of the people or the welfare of the animals. A couple of weeks later, I responded to a report from a lady who lived about four miles from the Orchard. She complained that Rambler ran alongside her car as she drove out of her long driveway. "He *chased* me!" she said. "He's *scaring* me!"

Rambler wasn't actually chasing her. He was only playing. He wasn't aggressive—*yet*. Upon further investigation with the neighbors, we learned that the lady had been feeding Rambler corn from a large platter set out behind her house. No wonder he was chasing her, he wanted more food!

Eventually Rambler got bored with apples and corn and started traveling again, looking for new adventures. He decided to hang out near a small tavern in the Del Rio area near the Tennessee-North Carolina border, just east of Newport, Tennessee. I got several calls over the weekend reporting that a moose was seen near the tavern.

Apparently some strong spirits were in use and had caused some patrons to mistake Rambler for a moose. He might've decided he was hanging out with the wrong crowd at the tavern, because he decided to change his ways. I got a report that he was seen near a Baptist Church on Sunday evening.

The following day, calls started coming in reporting that Rambler was near Hot Springs, North Carolina. Some people called and asked us to leave him there. Others wanted us to catch him and take him back to the Park so poachers wouldn't kill him. Some called just because they were excited to see him and wanted to let us know where he was.

Finally, I got a call from Mike Carraway who worked with the North Carolina Wildlife Resources Agency. Mike asked if I could come over and capture Rambler and take him back to Cataloochee. I asked Mike if the elk was doing anything wrong.

"Not really," he said, "but he's in North Carolina's *No Elk Zone*, and my phone is ringing off the wall."

Obviously we weren't the only ones getting calls about the wandering critter. Mike was right, we needed to go get Rambler, so we bundled up all our equipment and drove over to Hot Springs where we captured him, loaded him into a trailer, and hauled him back to Cataloochee.

Rambler stayed in Cataloochee over the following winter, spring, and summer, but in October, after the breeding season, called the *rut*, he started getting antsy again. Around Thanksgiving he hit the road and made his way back over to Tennessee to the exact same locations where he'd been fed by homeowners before.

It was a Sunday morning, and I was walking out of church to get in my pickup to go home, when I looked down at my cell phone and saw I had a message. Deep down inside, I didn't want to read the message. Getting a phone call while I was in church usually meant there was a wildlife problem somewhere that needed immediate attention. The previous week at work had been brutal and I needed some physical and mental rest. Apparently, I'd have to wait until later to get it.

I checked the message. It was Dispatch asking me to give them a call. They'd received a report from the Cocke County Sheriff's office saying that an elk was tangled in a swing near Carver's Orchard, in Cosby, Tennessee. Before I got home, the Sheriff's office called Dispatch again and asked if they should try and cut the elk loose. I told them, "No."

I knew it was Rambler and I intended to shorten his Tennessee vacation. In all his meanderings, crossing roads, yards, pastures, railroad tracks, parking lots, subdivisions, and more, I'd been terrified he'd be hit by a car and get injured or killed—or worse—injure or kill a person. It was time for the big fellow to go home, again.

It was a cold, blustery day, about 15-20 degrees, with a wind chill that drove the temperature down into the single digits.

On the way to the Park, I called Rick Varner and asked for his help. When I got to the Wildlife Building I hooked a horse trailer to the *Boar* truck, got some large and small darts, vials of immobilization drugs, two elk workup kits, an elk transport tarp, ropes, chains, saws, a tool kit, a net, the long and short range dart guns, a 30-06 caliber rifle, and potassium chloride for chemical euthanasia, in case that had to be done. On these kinds of trips, you have to take everything, because you never know what you'll need until you get there.

As I drove, I worried that I might've forgotten something. It was a long way to where the elk was struggling and I didn't have a clear idea about what sort of gear I was going to need when I got there.

I went to pick up Rick Varner at his house. His truck was being repaired and he had no wheels that day. I always felt better having Rick come along in any wildlife situation. No matter what the problem, he always seemed to come up with a solution.

When Rick and I arrived, we saw that Rambler was caught in the ropes of a homemade swing. The elk was struggling hard to get his antlers loose, but he couldn't break free. The ropes were hanging from a horizontal tree limb, and every time the elk lunged in one direction or the other, the whole tree would shake. I was concerned that the elk would break the ropes or the tree limb, or flip upside down and break his neck.

What complicated things even further was the location of the swing, it was on an earthen dam next to a small pond. If we didn't handle this just right, the elk was likely to fall off the pond side of the dam and drown, or fall off the other side which was a forty-five degree embankment. Either way, this was a risky location, for all of us.

I loaded a dart with the two elk immobilizations drugs, Carfentanil and Xylazine. Then I eased up to within twenty yards of the struggling animal and fired the dart. All we had to do now was wait five minutes or so and then we could start the process of untangling him and loading him in the trailer.

About four minutes after the drug was injected, Rambler started getting sleepy. After another minute his legs gave out and he collapsed, but his head was still being held by the ropes for the swing. I walked to with five yards of him to wait until he was fully immobilized. I noticed his stomach was jerking convulsively. I thought, *That's weird*. In the dozens of elk captures I'd been involved with, I'd never seen an elk do that before.

I needed to figure out what was going on, so I pulled his lip up to check the color of his gums. They should've been pink, which would indicate that the animal was getting a good oxygen supply. However,

Rambler's gums were purple.

Oh no! I realized he was choking to death. As his legs relaxed, the rope he was tangled in was tightening not just around his antler, but also around his neck.

He wasn't completely immobilized, but he couldn't breathe either. Something had to be done immediately! I asked Rick to cut him loose, even though I was worried he'd fall down the steep embankment and injure himself or roll off in the other direction toward the pond and drown.

We'd acquired an audience of police deputies, landowners, neighbors, and others watching to see how the *experts* would handle the big elk. It would be awful if we accidentally killed the elk while trying to rescue him.

Rick cut the rope and we both stood very still and were *extremely* quiet, hoping the elk wouldn't try to escape. The elk drew a huge breath into his lungs and was able to breathe normally again. He went to sleep very quickly after that. Rick and I were extremely relieved. We'd dodged a bullet on that one.

Four spectators helped and the six of us placed Rambler on the special elk tarp and then rolled him onto his chest and held him safely upright as Rick backed the truck onto the pond dam near to where Rambler was lying. We carefully slid the elk into our fourteen-foot horse trailer. I gave him the reversal drugs. Then Rick and I hauled him back to Cataloochee. We pulled the trailer up to a group of elk grazing in one of the fields.

When we opened the door Rambler ran out of the trailer. He was home again. The other elk were all looking at him. I'm sure when they saw him, they thought, "Oh, it's just Rambler. They've released him from jail, *again.*"

Rambler was definitely food-conditioned to people. He'd walk up driveways and into people's yards. After the incident with the rope swing he still did it, but now he made the trip back home to Cataloochee on his own each year. At first we worried about all his wandering because we didn't have confidence that he'd come back on his own. But he must've had the trail marked from Cataloochee to Cosby because he seemed to make the journey easily.

Then Rambler lost his radio-telemetry collar. For a while we had no way of tracking him and had no idea where he was. We looked, but didn't find him, and no one called to report his whereabouts. That was ominous. We wondered if he been killed by a poacher, or hit by a vehicle, or shot by a landowner who was tired of him eating their flowers.

It had been a couple of months since we'd had any contact with the elk, so we felt fairly sure that he was a goner. At times he'd been a pain to deal with, but you had to admire his spirit. He'd certainly provided some adventures for us. You get attached to any animal you handle as much as we did Rambler.

Then one morning, soon after I arrived at work, I got a call from Joe Yarkovich, the onsite wildlife manager of our elk herd. Joe lived in Cataloochee in the house that was traditionally allocated to the local ranger. He'd had replaced Steven Dobey, who'd become the bear and turkey biologist for the Kentucky Department of Wildlife Resources.

Joe called to let me know he'd found Elk #81. I pictured a decaying carcass or pile of bones. I asked Joe if he was dead. He laughed, and said, "No."

Early that morning at daylight, Joe said he'd heard an elk bugling in his front yard. That wasn't a normal occurrence. Bull elk do most of their bugling during the fall breeding season and that had ended a couple of months earlier. So, Joe got up and peeked through the blinds to see what was going on. He couldn't believe what he saw. It was Rambler, bugling his head off, standing in Joe's front yard letting everyone know he was back in town.

Joe said when he opened the blinds, Rambler stared at him as if to say, *You didn't think I could find my way back, did ya?*

THE WORST TRIP I'VE EVER BEEN ON

IN HINDSIGHT, it probably wasn't the best idea in the world to hire someone who had a bear phobia to man the frontlines in dealing with problem bears, but Emma O'Connell said it was what she wanted to do.

Emma was a university student in England who wanted to get some field experience with bears. She volunteered for a summer project in the Park. She sent me an email saying she'd been advised to come to the Smokies because it was the best place in the world for bear-people interactions.

We accepted her application and she came all the way from England for the opportunity to work with bears in the wild. I definitely provided her with some experience working with bears, but by accident, she got more than she bargained for.

Emma had straight, dark, shoulder length hair. She was a pretty girl, very fair skinned, and had an English accent that we all enjoyed hearing.

At that time it was our policy to have a Student Conservation Association intern or two go up and camp for at least two nights at any backcountry campsite that we'd closed for excessive bear activity before deciding whether or not it was safe to let the public back in. If there was no bear activity while the interns were there, we'd reopen the campsite. This policy seemed sensible to me at the time.

I sent Blake McCann and Emma to Backcountry Campsite #49 located on Bradley Fork about five miles above North Carolina's Smokemont Campground. Blake is a 6'5" rawboned country boy from Illinois. He can run up and down the Smokies trails like a racehorse. He's super-smart, honest, athletic, humble, strong as an ox—an All American Boy who wears size fourteen shoes.

Everything went well the first night. There was no bear activity.

So far, so good. But the second night was a different story. The second night there was *way* too much bear activity and neither Emma nor Blake was prepared for it. No one would've been.

Emma was a real sweet person, very polite and eager to help, and ready to experience new things. She definitely wasn't a hunter, though, and wouldn't hurt a flea. She was the kind of person who, if she saw a mouse inside a building, would use a live capture trap and take it outside so she could release it unharmed. If she saw a turtle crossing the road, she'd stop her car and move it off to the side so it wouldn't get run over. And she'd take injured animals to the vet if she saw one that had been hit in the road.

To be honest, Emma didn't seem to be cut out for field activities or working with wild animals, especially the big ones. In our correspondence before she arrived, she told me she had a fear of bears she was trying to overcome and she also said she had a fear of men from the South. From the things she'd read and seen on television and in the movies, she had the idea that most men from the South would literally run women down to catch them.

This was kind of comical to me and I tried to explain that this wasn't true in the Park, or in the surrounding areas. But I don't think she believed me. Anyway, she had these two deep fears running through her head before the real trouble even started.

On the second night at the Backcountry Campsite #49 Blake was sleeping in their small tent, and Emma was lying there next to him, wide awake at midnight, listening to all the wilderness sounds. At night in the backcountry, your imagination can run wild from all the things you hear outside your tent. It might be the snap of a twig, a limb crashing as it falls from a tree, the scream of a screech owl, a pack of coyotes howling, a fox barking, a grouse drumming, or nothing more than the wind blowing through the forest. Your mind can play tricks on you. Few campers sleep very well out there, except for Blake.

It was near midnight when Emma heard the sound of horses' hooves. They seemed to be coming down the trail, approaching the campsite. This particular campsite was at the end of a trail so there was nowhere else for people to go when they arrived there. All they could do was turn around and backtrack.

Emma realized it was the sound of several horses. People were riding in. She wondered why anyone would be riding horses in the middle of the night in the backcountry. She had no way to know it, but it was probably poachers, coming to a campsite they knew was closed to the public so they wouldn't be likely to encounter anyone. Campsite closures are widely advertised to the public, so it was well known to anyone who was interested in poaching that bears had been extremely active at the site for weeks.

Emma's mind started to race. She thought, *here come the Southern men.* She said the horses walked very close to the tent and then stopped. She could hear men mumbling, but couldn't understand what was being said. She said she was so scared she could barely breathe and that she was shaking inside her sleeping bag. Fortunately, whoever it was left after a few minutes. Blake slept through the whole thing.

Emma settled back down and tried to go to sleep, but with no luck. She lay there worrying that the Southern men on horses would return. She was finally dozing off when she realized she could hear something walking around the tent. Whatever it was, it was making moaning sounds and blowing noises. It was a bear!

The focus of her fears quickly changed from two-legged beasts to four-legged ones.

She lay perfectly still, hoping the bear would leave, but it didn't. The bear came right up to the tent and pushed against it with its nose, just above where Emma's head rested. Emma reached over and shook Blake, whispering, "Blake, wake up, there's a bear outside the tent!"

By now, the bear had walked around to Blake's side and was pushing against the tent near his feet. Barely awake and still very groggy, Blake sat up and forcefully backhanded the bear's snout through the thin nylon wall of the tent.

The bear jumped back and all was quiet for a few seconds. Emma said it seemed like an hour. But Blake's slap didn't have the intended result. The bear didn't leave the area.

Instead, after a few moments, it charged back and swatted at the tent, ripping it wide open. Then the bear stuck its head inside and clamped its jaws onto Blake, right through his sleeping bag. It grabbed him by his size fourteen foot.

The bear started dragging Blake out through the hole it had torn in the side of the tent.

It was pitch dark and they were being attacked by a full-sized adult black bear. Their lives were in serious danger. Both of them were screaming at the bear. Emma grabbed Blake by the arms and held on. The bear was on one end, pulling, and Emma was on the other. It was literally a tug of war and Blake was the prize!

Blake was kicking and yelling at the bear, but the big beast continued to slowly extract him from the tent. Luckily, Blake remembered the trusty Smith & Wesson .357 pistol in his backpack that he'd brought in case he needed to shoot a wild hog. He grabbed his backpack, pulled the pistol out, and fired a shot in the air in the hope that it might force the bear to break off its attack. His strategy worked.

After he fired the shot, the bear released him and slowly backed away. It didn't leave though, it only moved off to the edge of the campsite.

"I can't find my torch," Emma said. *Torch* is British English for flashlight.

They rummaged around in the wreckage of the tent for flashlights, still yelling at the bear. Gradually, with them both acting aggressive by shouting and throwing rocks, they finally managed to drive the bear away. It slowly disappeared into the darkness.

This encounter was a close one! That situation could easily have turned into the first human fatality in the history of the Park. But their determination to stay alive won out, with a little help from the loud racket of the pistol.

Why did the bear attack the tent and Blake? Was it after the food they'd stored up in a nearby tree? Was the bear predatory toward Blake and Emma? We'll never know for sure, but either way, this was about as serious a bear encounter as any camper could imagine.

The bear was gone for now, but neither of them knew what to do next. They faced a dilemma. Should they stay at the campsite for the rest of night, or should they pack up and hike five miles down the trail in the dark in the hope of finding help at Smokemont Campground?

There was no hesitation for Emma. She wanted to leave right away, take nothing, leave all the gear, and get the heck out of there. Blake wanted to pack everything and break camp the *right* way. He didn't want to leave anything for the bear to get, if it returned.

Emma didn't care about the bear, the tent, the packs, the clothes, the food, *anything*. She was focused on getting as far away as possible, as quickly as possible. They compromised. It was about one o'clock in the morning by the time they'd hastily crammed everything into their backpacks and hit the trail for the hike out of the backcountry.

They were agitated and annoyed with each other, so there wasn't much conversation as they made their way down to Smokemont

Campground. When they arrived, they were relieved to find a payphone at the campground. They each made a call to their group house behind Headquarters, but there was no answer at either one. Then they called Dispatch, but by then it was nearly 3 a.m. and Dispatch had gone home.

Smokemont Campground is situated between two rivers, the Oconaluftee and Bradley Fork. It sits on a flat piece of ground with a lot of trees. There's a horse camp near the entrance and a kiosk where campers check in when they arrive.

Blake and Emma decided the best thing to do was to find somewhere safe to sleep for a couple of hours. Having no keys to get into the kiosk, they decided to go inside the small stone building that housed the visitor's restrooms and wait there until daylight. Emma asked Blake to go into the women's side with her.

Blake lay down in the open area of the women's restroom with his feet under one of the stalls, and Emma sat in the far corner with her eyes wide open and her knees drawn up to her chest, clutching a hatchet with both fists.

I can't imagine how Blake was able to go to sleep beside a terrified woman who was holding a hatchet, but he did. I later asked him about this and he said, in his understated way, "I was just really tired and needed to get some sleep."

Blake was soon sound asleep. Emma kept her vigil alone until she heard something outside the building. She assumed the bear had followed them and was going to attack them again. She shook Blake awake for the second time that night. "Blake, wake up," she whispered, "I hear something. I think the bear's outside. He's followed us!"

This time Blake sprang into action immediately. He jumped up and whipped the restroom door open. He looked around, but he didn't see anything, so he came back inside and tried to calm Emma by saying that she was only hearing things. He suggested she try to get some sleep.

That was not about to happen, of course. But, in an effort to re-assure her, Blake took the precaution of wedging his backpack under the restroom door from the inside, using it as a doorstop. Then he lay back down again and went back to sleep.

At about 6 a.m. it still wasn't quite daylight. Emma had actually managed to doze off when she heard something outside and looked up to see the restroom door moving. Something was trying to get inside.

"Blake!" she said, "Wake up, the bear is trying to come through the door."

So, for the third time that night, Blake roused from a deep sleep. He saw the door jerking, got up quietly and crept over to it. He gathered all his strength and then hauled off and kicked the door as hard as he could with his size fourteen boots, hoping to scare away the bear the other side.

The door flew open and a shape went flying backward and hit the ground. But it wasn't a bear. It was a small elderly lady. She'd been shoving at the door, trying to get it open.

When Blake ran over to help her, she looked up at him in confusion, and said, "I just wanted to go to the bathroom."

Blake apologized, and said, "Well come on in, Ma'am."

"No, thank you," she said, "I think I'll go over to the men's side."

Later, when Dispatch returned to duty, they sent someone to pick up Blake and Emma and bring them to Headquarters. When they arrived, both of them were still in shock. Who wouldn't be?

During my long talk with Emma, she asked, "Are there any churches in this area?"

I told her there were several.

"I'd like to go to church this Sunday," she said.

I told her she was welcome to come with me to my Baptist Church. But she said she was Catholic, so I set her up with my boss, Carroll Schell, who was Catholic.

Still shaken from the ordeal, Emma tried to explain the details of the incident. I was really worried about her. She'd experienced a bear attack that could affect her forever. I looked at her and asked, "Emma, are you okay?"

"I'm much better now," she said, "but it was a struggle to hold myself together as we fled from the campsite. I spoke to God and my mum quite a bit on that hike down to Smokemont."

Apparently, some promises were made, too. Emma went to church every single Sunday until she returned to England.

I encouraged her to stay at the Park and work with other departments to gain additional experience, but she wanted to go home. For the rest of the time she was at the Park, she would never go out of her dorm at night unless she was with either me or Rick Varner. She was still living in fear of what had happened, and even worse, what could've happened.

Blake was really worried he might be in trouble for not doing a better job of protecting Emma, for firing his pistol to scare the bear, and for kicking a little old lady down at the restroom. But he wasn't.

I was so thankful that Blake had been there and that neither of them had been alone that night. I was sorry about what happened to them. But, if it had been a solo camper or a family with young children in that tent, I don't want to think what might've happened.

When Emma got home she emailed me from England to thank me for hiring her. I told her that because of what had happened to her and Blake, I was changing the way we monitored a closed back-country campsite. In the future, we'd use remote cameras to check for bear activity instead of sending people out to spend the night at the site. That policy is still in place today.

In one of the last email exchanges I had with Emma, I asked her if she intended to continue her bear research. She said she'd like to, but only on the computer and never again in the field.

ELK RODEO

ANY OF THE WILDLIFE RANGERS you ask will probably say that one of the worst days you can have at work is when you're trying to capture a wild animal and you miss a shot with the dart rifle. It's especially bad when this happens in front of a big crowd of Park visitors.

It may not sound like a big deal, but it is. It's embarrassing and humiliating. Your confidence flies out the window and you just want to crawl in a hole.

It's not easy to dart a wild animal. There are so many things that can go wrong, and any little mistake can mess everything up. But to effectively manage large wild animals, we need to be able to get our hands on them.

They need to be fully immobilized, or anesthetized, before you can get close enough to examine them, give them medical care, put a research radio-collar on them, or transport them. So, the skill to use immobilization drugs to capture bears, elk, or deer is very important

I'm kind of like Barney Fife in that I usually take only one dart with me when I go after a bear or an elk. If it's an elk, it usually takes most of a day to plan and get everything ready to try and capture it.

When first learning to dart an animal in front of a crowd, some rangers get so nervous they're shaking like a leaf. In my early years, I certainly did.

It can take a lot of time and luck to get a good shot at an animal. The elk darts have a short barb on the needle so they'll stay in and not bounce off, or fall out. But if the animal moves just a little bit at the last instant, or if there's a crosswind, the dart can miss its mark.

I darted a yearling female elk in Cataloochee once in a crosswind and unfortunately the dart struck the animal's rib cage. This isn't a good injection site. You could break a rib or cause some internal damage. Fortunately, neither of those things happened in this case.

Although the dart hit the elk, and stayed in, the elk didn't go down. Sometimes this happens. The elk continued to walk around in the Cataloochee fields with the brightly colored yellow dart dangling from its side.

It doesn't cause any harm to the elk, but tourists called the rangers, the rangers called Dispatch, and Dispatch called me—dozens of times, about that one elk.

For a couple of weeks, I made trips over the mountain to try and find the elk so I could remove the dart, but I couldn't get within a hundred yards of her. She wasn't about to stand around and let me shoot her again. Every time I got out of my vehicle and even *tried* to get close to her, she took off across the field and wouldn't stop until she was a couple of hundred yards away. Then she'd stand there, staring at me.

I can guess what she was thinking.

I wanted to get the dart out, but the elk wouldn't have anything to do with me anymore, and I don't blame her. Finally, the dart fell out on its own.

A few weeks later we were able to dart her and place a radio collar on her so we could track her movements. We thoroughly examined her while she was immobilized. She was in good physical shape. Probably better than me. When I reversed her, she ran off about forty yards and turned around to look at us. Again, I could probably guess what she was thinking and I'm sure it wasn't positive thoughts about me. All she wanted was for us to leave her alone.

Another memorably bad day was when I was trying to catch Elk

#40, a three year old female that had wandered outside the Park and onto a farm where she wasn't wanted. My attempt to capture her turned into a disaster.

I was waiting in a tree stand at the top of an extremely steep hill, hoping to be able to dart the wayward elk. I needed to catch her and take her back to the Park as soon as possible.

As I sat in the tree, I could hear something walking in the leaves below me, heading my way. Soon, I saw Elk #40 cautiously easing her way up the fencerow near where I was sitting. I quietly loaded the dart into my dart rifle and slowly closed the lever, locking the dart in place. As the elk got closer, I carefully raised the rifle and rested the scope crosshairs on the center of her right front shoulder and slowly squeezed the trigger.

She immediately wheeled and ran back down the hill and out of sight. The shot placement was perfect, though, so I was congratulating myself. All I had to do now, I thought, was walk down the hill and find Ole #40 sleeping soundly.

When I'd packed everything up, I walked down the hill looking for the elk, expecting her to be lying somewhere nearby. Still patting myself on the back for a job well done, I thought I'd turn my Park radio on to call Jennifer Murrow to let her know that I'd darted the elk perfectly and was heading downhill to look for her. But, instead, when I turned the radio on, the first thing I heard was Jennifer screaming, "They're stampeding toward the Interstate."

I wondered *what* was stampeding toward the Interstate?

"Jennifer," I asked, "what's going on?"

She screamed back, "There's a herd of cattle stampeding through the pasture, tearing down fences and heading toward Interstate 40!"

I was confused. What did cattle stampeding have to do with me darting an elk? I ran down the hill as fast as I could. When I got to the bottom, I saw Barry Holbert, a Rocky Mountain Elk Foundation volunteer who was helping us.

"Barry, did you see the elk?" I asked.

He nodded. He said she ran down the hill, stopped, looked at him for a moment, then bolted over the fence into a farmer's pasture that contained some young Holstein heifers.

Holsteins can be a little spirited and this group was definitely of the high-strung variety. Barry said Elk #40 jumped the fence near where the cattle were standing. This scared them and started a stampede.

I thought to myself, *This is not good.*

Apparently, the tranquilizer dart hadn't discharged and injected the drug into the elk, so the animal didn't go to sleep. Instead, it continued to run, herding the terrified cows toward nearby Interstate 40. In their panicked stampede, the animals broke down three fences. It was a nightmare.

Barry and I ran to our vehicle and took off down the road looking for the fleeing cattle. I didn't know where Elk #40 had gone, and frankly didn't care at the moment. My focus was now on preventing the farmer's cattle from running up onto the Interstate and causing an accident. Barry and I drove over the hill and saw a small group of cattle hurtling through a wheat field heading directly toward the Interstate.

I tore down the road and managed to get in front of the lead cow. Barry and I jumped out of the SUV. Barry was younger, smaller, and much faster than I. He took off toward the cattle like an Australian Blue Heeler cattle dog. Barry was a good cowman and he was able to head the cattle off and turn them around before they ran up the entrance ramp and onto I-40. That would've been the worst thing *ever.* Then Barry and I shepherded all the cattle back into an adjacent pasture where they eventually settled down.

That's how quickly a triumph can turn into a disaster when you're working with large wild animals. I was learning humility the hard way. Over the years, I'd told our visitors thousands of times that wildlife in the Smokies have behaviors that are sometimes unpredictable. Well, this was definitely one of those times. I got a firsthand lesson in how unpredictable they can be.

The following week, Jennifer and I found Elk #40 about half a mile from where the cattle stampede fiasco had happened. One of the locals told us that the elk had been traversing his pasture to eat from a mineral block that he put out for his goats. The block also had corn and molasses mixed in, which was probably what attracted the elk. The molasses smelled really good.

It took a couple of evenings to learn the elk's behavior pattern, but on the second evening I was able to dart her and haul her back to Cataloochee. I hoped she'd stay put this time because I wasn't sure how many more rodeos I could take.

🐾　🐾　🐾　🐾　🐾

Working in front of a large crowd of tourists can add a lot of stress to any task. I sent one of our best wildlife rangers to capture a bear that was begging for food near the Thomas Divide Trailhead on Hwy. 441 in North Carolina. A couple of hours later, I got a radio call from him. He was obviously upset. He asked to meet me in my office. "Sure," I said, "come on."

As soon as he walked through the door, he threw his arms in the air, and said, "I'm fired."

"Why?" I asked.

"It's on video," he said. "The whole thing's on video, and on a *lot* of cameras."

"What's on video?"

"I was trying to dart the bear you sent me after. It attracted a big audience and I mean *a really big* audience.

"I worked with the bear for a long time before I finally got it into a safe spot away from cars, the people, and the cliffs. I was set up for a perfect shot, but I *missed*. The dart flew over the bear's back.

"When I realized I'd missed, I couldn't believe it. I let out a string of curse words that echoed for miles. There must've been seventy-five people there who heard, and saw, and filmed the whole thing."

Rangers weren't supposed to swear, especially not in front of a big crowd of Park visitors. He and I waited nervously for any fallout, but no one ever complained.

Now he has my job.

HOGS GONE WILD

AS PART OF THE ANNUAL orientation and training for the Resource Education staff, the rangers who teach visitors about the Park's natural and cultural resources, I was asked to give a talk on the topic of wild hog control to about thirty Park employees.

It just so happened that we'd trapped an adult wild hog the morning of the seminar. That was lucky, I thought, because props, especially live ones, always added an extra dimension to any presentation. I hoped that by adding a live animal to my talk, I'd improve the rangers' retention of the information I was going to give them.

We assembled near the entrance to the Elkmont Nature Trail where I had a 130-pound hog in a trap. The area around the trap had been rooted up and heavily damaged by the beasts. I gave my audience a lot of statistics about how many wild hogs were in the Park, how many we'd removed over the years, and what sort of damage the hogs would do if we didn't keep the population under control.

Pigs are the most prolific large mammal in North America. In some ways, they're like a big, ugly rabbit, capable of having two litters a year. Research indicates that we need to remove about half of the wild hogs every year to keep the population levels under control. If not, their numbers grow in a hurry.

The hog reduction program began in the late 1950s. In all the years from the late 50s to the late 70s combined, approximately 1,000 hogs were removed from the Park. Back then, we used to donate the hogs we trapped to the states of Tennessee and North Carolina so they could relocate them to state-controlled areas where the public could hunt them. Today, because of the concern over spreading diseases, we no longer do that.

During the thirty-two years of my career, the wild hog control crews have reduced the population by another 12,000 animals. We used to trap a lot of them with cages, but now there are fewer hogs and they're more spread out. So these days we trap less and shoot more, but that varies from year to year depending on how many piglets are born, and the availability of food, mainly acorns.

In 1986 I was given extra funding to address the hog problem and we removed 1,146 pigs in that year. That was the most hogs ever removed in a single year and still holds the record today. In subsequent years we removed anywhere from about 200 to 700. Nowadays it's more like 250 to 300 a year.

I was explaining to the teaching rangers about the hogs' eating habits, how to locate them, and how to identify the signs that they've been in the area. I demonstrated the firearms and the specialized equipment we used for night hunting.

Then I talked about trapping. I explained how we set traps, baited them, and then, when we caught a hog, how we transported it. For the grand finale, I wanted to show the group how to transfer a wild hog from a trap into a portable transfer cage so we could load the critter into a truck or a boat and then haul it out of the Park.

Without thinking very much in advance, as usual, I talked confidently, explaining, "We use shelled corn for bait, which means that our bait will attract any animal that likes corn—like a bear, deer, turkey, or raccoon. So we have a nine-inch square opening cut into the top of every trap. It's a hole in the chain link that non-target animals can use to get out if they get trapped inside."

Then I started my demonstration of how we transferred a hog from one cage to another.

"First," I said, "I'm gonna restrain the hog by reaching through the escape hatch in the top of the cage and carefully placing a lasso around the hog's neck," I said, as I lowered the noose through the small opening in the top of the cage. Of course, the hog wasn't happy about the situation. He was upset about being trapped and also about having a crowd of people around him. I'm sure he wanted to get the heck out of Dodge and I knew he would've liked to put the hurt on me or anyone else if he got the opportunity.

These hybrid wild hogs can be really mean and aggressive.

The hog was jumping around, blowing, popping its jaws, and gnashing its teeth. It was making an eerie groaning sound and would occasionally charge and hit the side of the trap with so much force that the entire five-by-five-foot cage would hop across the ground a few inches. All I needed was music from *Jaws* and the stage would've been set for a horror movie.

The purpose of putting a lasso on the hog was to restrain it just long enough so I could open the door, grab hold of its back legs, drag it out, and put it in the transfer cage. It didn't hurt the hog at all, but it frightened him and made him even more aggressive than usual, which is saying something.

Once I had the rope around the hog's neck, I tightened it. When I did, the hog started leaping around like it was on a trampoline. Holding the rope felt like trying to land a 100-pound catfish with a ten-foot cane pole. I yelled at Pete, a wildlife intern from Canada, and asked him to hold the rope tight so I could open the door and grab the hog. I explained to Pete how important it was for him to hold that rope tight. If he didn't, someone could get hurt, and more than likely that person would be me.

Pete wasn't a big guy. He weighed about 150 pounds. This was the first time he'd ever been asked to restrain a wild hog and he was obviously a little unsure about what to expect. He was eager to do whatever I asked, but if I'd thought about it a little more in advance, I would've realized that there was no way in the world Pete could restrained an angry wild hog that weighed nearly as much as he did.

This hog was highly motivated to use his sharp tusks to cut me or anybody else in the area. He also had four feet on the ground for traction, and we had only two. Nevertheless, I handed Pete the rope and told him to hold on tight. Then I walked around to the front of the cage and positioned myself beside the front door so I could raise it, grab the hog's back feet, and pull it out of the trap.

By now, the entire group of rangers had moved in close to get a better look. Handling fierce, angry, wild animals barehanded was *nothing* like what they were accustomed to doing or seeing. They were standing in a semi-circle around the door of the cage, watching intently for what was about to happen next.

To speed up the process of transferring a wild hog from one cage to another, we normally just grabbed the hog, pulled it out, and stuck it in the transfer cage. It wasn't the safest or smartest way to handle the pig, but was the quickest.

The rangers were slightly bent over, eyes glued to the trap door. I had a captive audience. I hoped I'd be able to keep the hog captive, too. I was in my element and was really proud of myself. But, what happened next was certainly a surprise to all of us, including the hog.

I got down on one knee and carefully began to slide the trap door up, but the hog's rear end was pressing hard against it, which made it hard to open. I was in a strain trying to get into a decent position to grab the hog's back legs. I was able to reach in, but when I grabbed the hog's legs, it jerked free of my grip and exploded toward the other end of the cage where Pete was standing.

Now I was able to get the door up so the front of the trap was completely open. At this stage of the process, I was supposed to be holding on the hog's rear legs, but unfortunately I wasn't. The hog did a gymnastic flip in the air, and blasted out of the cage like a rocket heading for the moon.

Pete was so shocked by the hog's reaction, he relaxed his grip on the rope. It zipped through his hands like a big blue marlin stripping fishing line off a reel. When Pete saw the hog clear the trap, he began to understand the importance of holding onto the rope, so he clamped down on it immediately and wrapped it around a small tree next to where he was standing. That stopped the hog's charge. The hog had made it about ten feet outside the trap when the lasso around its neck arrested its escape.

When the rope suddenly tightened, it caused the animal to rear up on its high legs. The hog did a wheelie right into the faces of the rangers in the front row. The furious pig was grunting and squealing and making all sorts of horrible sounds. While it was reared up on its hind legs, I jumped up from where I was kneeling, threw myself onto the hog, grabbing it from behind in a big bear (or hog) hug, restraining it.

The hog and I both fell to the ground. Pete then leaped onto the hog too, to help prevent it from getting up. During the chaos, I'd completely forgotten about our class of rangers.

Their response to the fiasco was priceless. I looked up from where I lay on the ground wrestling with the hog, and saw rangers scattering in every direction, running for their lives. It was one of the funniest sights I've ever seen in my life. I had to laugh even though I was still grappling with the crazed wild hog.

Laughing was better than crying.

I could've done either at this point. This was extremely embarrassing for me. If Pete hadn't been able to stop the hog's charge before it got to the group, it would have literally run over several of them. Not a good situation.

I wasn't the only one who should've been ashamed, though. All thirty of the rangers had taken off into the surrounding woods. By the time I got the hog secured and had a chance to look around, all I could see was waving leaves and trembling tree limbs. There had been a few screams, some utterances I can't repeat, and a lot of yelling, but I can assure you that not a single one of the rangers came back to help me and Pete. It was every man and woman for themselves, and I frankly don't blame them.

Then I noticed one fellow who was still partially visible through the brush. It was a young man who was crawling away faster than I'd ever seen anybody move on their hands and knees. Apparently he'd fallen or been knocked down during the rangers' stampede and he didn't want to take the time to stand up, so he just continued on all fours, crawling the entire way across the clearing and off into the woods on all fours.

His arms and legs were working so fast it looked like he was in a video set on fast forward. There's no doubt in my mind that a video of my presentation would've won the $10,000 prize on *America's Funniest Home Videos*.

An especially comical aspect of the situation was that not all of the people who ran were trainees. Most of them were seasonal employees who worked just during the times of highest visitation, but some of them were high-ranking Park staff. But on that day, at that time, neither your status, your department, nor your job title played any part in the retreat. The one and only objective of the group when the hog charged out of the trap was to put some space between them and the crazed animal. They did an excellent job.

When I realized I'd been deserted by everyone but trusty Pete, I jokingly shouted toward the woods, "Don't worry guys. We're okay! You can all go back to your vehicles!"

Pete and I looked at each other and burst out laughing.

The two of us finally managed to put the hog into the transfer cage and we carried it to the truck and loaded it by ourselves. When we got to the parking area, the teaching rangers were sitting in their vehicles watching us, bug-eyed. I suspected a few calls had already been made to Park Dispatch or maybe even 911.

Once we had the hog in the back of my truck, I yelled out to the group asking if they wanted to get out of their vehicles and let me finish my lecture.

"Nope, I think we're all good," said the leader, "It's time for us to be heading on back now."

I walked over to where he was sitting in the driver's seat of one of the vehicles and apologized for the mishap and assured him that this sort of thing didn't happen very often. I said I still had more information to give the rangers about hogs but he made it clear that the class was over.

Even if I'd offered them winning lottery tickets, I don't think a single one of them would've gotten out of their vehicles again.

As the group drove off, I thought more about the various percentages of information an audience retained from different types of presentations. I was pretty sure that the addition of the live hog insured that every one of those rangers would retain an unusually high percentage of what they'd seen that day. I know I did.

HOGGING THE CAMERA

WE SHOULD'VE LEARNED our lesson after the fiasco when we'd allowed a television crew to accompany us into the back-country to film our attempt to capture and relocate a mother bear and her cub. Things hadn't gone well, to say the least.

And then we'd had the episode of the teaching ranger presentation gone horribly awry.

So when I got a call from Nancy Gray, a Public Affairs Officer for the Park, asking me to take CNN with me to film a segment on wild hogs in the Park, I should've known better. I wasn't crazy about the idea, but I figured if I kept the hog in the cage the whole time, what could go wrong?

We wanted to show the CNN crew the impact of wild hogs on the Park, so we drove them around and looked at several damaged areas. We even allowed them to go with us as we checked hog traps, in the hope that we'd catch a hog and have something interesting to look at besides just messy, muddy ruts plowed up by the pesky creatures.

We checked the traps near Headquarters with no luck, but then I got a call from one of our guys who was checking traps in Cades Cove. He said he'd captured an old 150-pound boar in a trap and could bring him over to Headquarters, if that would help. The CNN crew was leaving later that day and they didn't have time for a round-trip drive to Cades Cove, so I asked for the trapped hog to be brought over.

The film crew and several wildlife handlers were waiting at the Wildlife Building when the hog arrived in the trap. I noticed the trap was an extremely old model. It was a type used back in the 70s. It was seven-feet long, three-and-a-half feet high, and about three-feet wide. It was framed out of round galvanized pipe and covered with heavy-gauge chain link fencing. The door was made of three-quarter inch plywood and reinforced with crisscrossing metal strips.

Although the trap was old, it still appeared to be fairly sturdy. I was a little nervous. The one thing I desperately wanted to avoid was for any of us to do or say anything dumb while CNN was filming. This was our chance to show people across the entire country how we managed large wild critters. Unfortunately, the demonstration didn't turn out exactly as I'd hoped.

The wildlife technicians unloaded the hog trap from the *Shoat* truck and set it in a grassy area just behind the Wildlife Building near the Two Mile Trail and the West Prong of the Little Pigeon River. It was obvious that this 150-pound porker was furious about his situation. He wanted to hurt someone, anyone. He kept lunging at us, grunting, blowing, and popping his jaws. I was thankful he was in a trap. I would've hated to run across him out in the Park in the middle of the night.

I stood beside the trap as CNN filmed an interview with me about wild hogs, our hog control program, and the problems that hogs caused in the Park. The whole time I was talking it was very easy to see that the wild boar was becoming more and more enraged. It was leaping and snorting inside the cage.

When we finished with the interview, I told the guys they could reload the hog. It should've been a simple task—pick up the trap, slide it into the bed of the truck, and off they'd go. We'd be finished, mission accomplished, a job well done.

When the cameraman was ready, the wildlife crew sprang into action. Unbeknownst to me and everyone but the hog, there was a small break in the chain link on the bottom of the cage. We hadn't seen it, but the hog had, and he'd been waiting for just this moment. When we lifted the cage off the ground, the hog put everything he had into enlarging the small hole as quickly as possible.

The guys got one end of the trap set on the back of the truck, but before they could slide it the rest of the way in, the wild hog exploded through the bottom of the cage like a torpedo out of a submarine. In a flash, he made his escape and tore across the small grassy clearing, heading toward the deep dark forest.

He ran about thirty yards, then in true *Rooshin* style, he stopped, turned, and looked back at us. He was obviously thinking homicidal thoughts. Then he changed his mind about running away. He decided to come back and extract some revenge. This notorious ferocity is one of the reasons why handling or hunting hogs is so dangerous.

All the animal had to do was run a few more yards and he'd have disappeared into the thick brush. He would've been free. Of course, I would have been embarrassed and my pride would've taken a hit, but I'd have gotten over it.

But *nooooo*, the wild hog galloped straight toward us. He was in full charge and the attack was on. I'm not sure how fast that wild hog was running, but I'm sure there was no one in our group who could've outrun him. We all needed to get out of the way immediately.

I knew the hog would be especially interested in settling the score with me. Unfortunately I happened to be the farthest away from the truck. I turned to make a dash for safety and noticed that the bed of the truck was already full of people. I wondered how in the world everybody else got up in there so fast. Obviously extreme fear and adrenaline gave some people superhuman speed.

I ran closer because there was no other choice, and realized the bed of the truck was jammed *completely* full of people and equipment, to the point that there was *zero* room for me—none. It didn't matter anyway, though, because time had run out. The hog was on me.

At a time like this, you find out who your friends really are. I've always heard that a real friend is someone who would do *anything* for you, any time or any place, no matter what the circumstances. A true friend would even *die* for you.

It didn't look like I had any true friends in this group.

I turned to face the hog as he charged me. He tried to bite me and cut my legs. With my bare hands, I slapped his ears and then his head as hard as I possibly could. He was grunting every time I slapped him, but in no way was I deterring him. The image of his wide open mouth, with those huge curved tusks on either side, was burned into my brain forever.

Those tusks hadn't looked as big when the hog was inside the cage, but they sure looked big now, especially when they were grazing the sides of my legs. I hopped from one foot to the other to keep the hog from goring me. If he managed to stab me with one of his tusks, and then jerked his head, I'd get a horrible injury. I wanted to kick him, but I had to keep both feet moving all the time or he would've torn me wide open.

The attack had been going on for just a few seconds when one of our young wildlife interns, Alan Loy, made a move as if to jump down and help me. Alan told me later that one thought kept running through his mind, *Kim's gonna get cut to pieces if somebody doesn't do something.*

Alan said he decided to jump out of the truck so he could try to scare the hog away. But just as he started to leap off the tailgate to help me, he heard a voice inside his head shout, *Alan, are you crazy?*

He said the voice stopped him. He paused, thought about helping me, then said out loud, "Sorry, not me, boys!"

Thank goodness there was one guy in the truck who would decide otherwise. That person was Rick Varner. It didn't surprise me that of all the people who were there that day, Rick would be the one who'd place himself in mortal danger to help me. Very few people in this world would willingly intervene in a fight with a deadly, vicious wild animal. But Rick Varner is that kind of man—even though he could've been slashed and gored and bled to death. He'd do it for me, you, or anybody in trouble.

An instant before Rick jumped out of the truck, he reached down and grabbed one of the galvanized pipes we used to carry the hog traps. Then he leaped out and charged straight toward the wild hog. When Rick approached him, the wild boar stopped attacking me and immediately turned to focus on Rick. Good for me, but bad for Rick.

The beast lunged toward Rick, tossing his head back and forth savagely, trying to slash him with his tusks. Boar tusks were always kept razor sharp because each time a hog's teeth bit together, the tusks slid across each other and sharpened themselves like a pair of scissors.

Before Rick could stop him, the hog sliced open the leg of his trousers from the back of his knee up to his hip. When I saw that, I thought Rick had been cut bad. I hoped one of the spectators would have the presence of mind to call 911.

After the hog slashed Rick's pants open, it turned and bolted, charging across the river. I've never been so happy to see the rear end of a hog in all my life. I was extremely relieved that the horrible attack was over, but dreaded to see what price Rick had paid to save me.

Everyone jumped out of the truck and ran toward Rick. "Let me see your leg," I gasped.

Rick turned around. I expected to see a lot of blood, but instead, through the gaping hole in the back of his Park Service pants we could see a foot-long bright red mark up the back of his leg. It looked like someone had taken a red magic marker and drawn a long straight line up the back of his thigh. Miraculously the hog's tusk hadn't broken the skin. It was just a terrible scratch.

By some phenomenal bit of good luck, or the grace of God, no one was seriously hurt. As I looked around, I noticed the CNN crew. During the attack I'd completely forgotten about them. Then I realized the camera guy was still filming! CNN had never turned the camera off. They'd filmed the entire attack.

I couldn't believe it.

When we'd all calmed down, I walked over to the cameraman and asked as casually as I could, "Hey, ahhhh, whaddya think they'll do with that footage."

He shook his head, and said, "Probably nothing."

I thought, *Yeah, right.* The camera guy knew he'd just filmed something a lot more exciting than what they'd originally hoped to get. I found out a couple of weeks later that they aired the hog attack footage nationwide.

I know this because a friend of mine called me from Washington State to say he'd seen me in an interview on CNN. He was laughing so hard he could barely talk. So much for looking professional on national television.

At least everyone got a chuckle out of it. It's funny now, but let me tell you, I sure didn't see anyone laughing during the attack. The day after the incident the Park Superintendent, Randy Pope, called me into his office. "Kim," he said, "I don't think we should ever do that again."

I agreed wholeheartedly.

No matter what the animal, time of year, location, or procedure—no more television crews would *ever* be allowed to film us working with wild animals again. No way, no exceptions.

A BRUSH WITH DEATH

MANY OF THE PREDATORY black bear attacks on humans are directed toward the smallest person in a group—either a child or the smallest adult. Additional factors that indicate a bear attack on a human might be of a predatory nature are:

- the attack is persistent
- human food doesn't appear to be involved
- the attack generally occurs around May or October
- the black bear is a male
- there's no prior history of the animal misbehaving
- the attack occurs in the daytime

It's important to understand that black bear attacks usually differ from attacks by other species of bears, and the correct response to them differs as well. Many people in the South never consider that our black bears might look at people as prey for their next meal. That's because black bears almost never do this.

Predatory black bear attacks are extremely rare. But we still need to remember that sometimes black bears *do* look at a person as a potential source of food.

In August of 2008, Evan Pala, an eight-year-old boy from Boca Raton, Florida, was attacked by an eighty-six-pound, male black bear 300 yards up the Rainbow Falls Trail from the parking area. Evan was visiting the Park with his father, John, and his older brother, Alex.

It was 7:30 p.m. and Evan had been playing in the small Le Conte Creek and was scrambling up a bank ahead of his father and brother when he encountered a bear. Evan's brother said they'd just started to make their way back to their vehicle when he glanced up and saw a bear pop up behind Evan.

The bear placed both of its front feet on the back of Evan's shoulders and started riding him down to the ground. Evan screamed.

As the boy was falling down with the bear on his back, Alex said he could see the bear's mouth wide open, going for Evan's shoulders and neck. Evan's father heard the boy's scream and ran over to find the bear on top of his son.

Evan's father grabbed the bear's jaws with his bare hands and pried them open. Then he yelled, beat, and shoved the bear, trying to get the beast off of Evan and stop the attack. John finally got the bear off his son and told Evan to run. The boy managed to get up, and he tried to run away, but he tripped.

The bear stayed focused on Evan and ran after him. He pounced on the boy for a second time in a persistent attack. Evan's father intervened again, fighting the bear, and managed to pull the animal off his son for a second time. This time Evan was able to escape. As he ran, his father and brother yelled, and screamed, and threw rocks and sticks at the bear. They managed to make the bear move back, but it didn't leave the area.

Evan's father and brother backed away from the bear slowly. When they were about twenty feet away, they turned and ran. In a few minutes they made it back to the parking lot where they'd left their car and found Evan waiting for them. He was bruised, cut, scratched, and bitten.

The boy's most severe injuries were lacerations and bite marks to the back of his neck and tops of his shoulders. His father had minor cuts on his right hand and bruises on his feet. He'd also lost his shoes when wrestling with the bear.

Gatlinburg Emergency Medical Services responded to a 911 call. Dispatch was notified and a call was made to the on-duty law enforcement rangers. Rangers Johnson and Biggs came to the parking lot where they found the EMT's working on Evan and his father. The rangers talked with Mr. Pala about the attack and where it happened. Then Evan was transported by ambulance to Fort Sanders Sevier Medical Center in Sevierville, Tennessee for treatment.

Bill Stiver was at home when he got the call about the attack. He called me to relay the details. He said a couple of our wildlife guys were already on their way up to the Rainbow Falls parking area with a bear trap. After the ambulance took off for the hospital, Rangers Johnson and Biggs walked up to the scene of the attack. On the way to the creek, they found a green ball cap and a white sneaker.

While they were searching along the creek, a family hiking down the trail stopped to ask what they were doing. The rangers explained that they were looking for a bear that had attacked a young boy. While they were talking, a man in the family shouted that there was a bear behind them. The two rangers turned around and sure enough, the bear was approaching them, walking rapidly.

The bear was about thirty feet away from them, but was coming toward them fast. The animal made no noises or vocalizations. It wasn't swatting the ground, blowing, moaning, or popping its jaws. The absence of warning sounds, or any noise, indicated the bear was behaving *offensively*, meaning it was either after their food, or was after *them*.

In light of what had just taken place, the attack on Evan, I believe the bear was after the people. The rangers felt they had no choice but to raise their weapons and put the animal down. They shot the bear as it continued to close in on them.

Ranger Chuck Hester took the bear to University of Tennessee Veterinary Hospital for a *necropsy*, a post-mortem exam on the animal. This revealed that the bear had meningitis, an inflammation of the protective membranes surrounding the brain and spinal cord. This may have been a factor in the bear's aggressive behavior, but we'll never know for sure.

The bear tested negative for rabies. In the animal's stomach, they found blue and white material which turned out to be part of an insole from a shoe. Also, there was a piece of leather with a logo on it. The rangers were able to match the material found in the bear's stomach with a shoe John Pala had lost while fighting the bear. Ranger Hester also identified some natural foods in the stomach such as huckleberries, blueberries, and insects. It was perfectly clear that this bear was the one that had attacked Evan.

The Pala family had eaten Kentucky Fried Chicken about an hour before the attack, but there was no food present during the attack itself. The bear had no history of problem behavior. This was a persistent attack by a male bear that occurred in the daytime. All these factors indicate to me that it was a predatory attack.

Evan was very lucky to be alive. If he'd been hiking alone or been farther away from his father, things could've turned out much worse. This was a close one. Evan was one lucky boy. His brave father and brother had saved his life.

🐾 🐾 🐾 🐾 🐾

Stephen Herrero, author of the book *Bear Attacks: Their Causes and Avoidance*, says at least sixty-three people have been killed by black bears in North America since 1900. Forty-six of those deaths were in Alaska or Canada. Only one known death has ever occurred in the Great Smoky Mountains National Park as the result of a black bear attack.

COLD DAY IN BIG SOUTH FORK

WE WERE HELPING with a University of Tennessee research project where we donated black bears to Big South Fork National River and Recreation Area in an effort to reestablish them there.

We were trying to learn whether bears were more likely to stay put after relocation if we moved single bears or mother bears with their cubs.

On this extremely cold February day, eight hardy souls were moving a mother bear with newborn cubs. The family was taken out of their den, which was located near Parson Branch Road in the west end of the Park. This is a narrow, primitive, one-way, eight-mile-long road with eighteen creek fords.

The road had been heavily damaged by floods and was impassible for vehicles, so we couldn't drive in. We had to hike for about two miles from a section of Hwy. 129 known as the *Tail of the Dragon*, a famous 11-mile stretch of mountainous highway with 318 curves that was a favorite of recreational motorcyclists. The ground was covered with snow and it was very cold.

The University of Tennessee has been researching bears in the Smokies for over thirty years. They wanted to know where bears slept and what they ate. Bears aren't easy to locate in the rough terrain of the Park.

The researchers placed radio tracking collars on a few dozen bears, mainly adult females, so they could learn where they denned and how many cubs they had. The radio collars allowed us to find the bears and their dens relatively easily. The key word here is *relatively*.

The denning behavior of bears in the Smokies is different from bears in other areas of the country. Many of our bears use dens that are high off the ground. The old den tree we were looking for was a couple of hundred yards off the road in a huge oak. It was on an extremely steep slope that was covered with ice and snow. As we walked, people were regularly slipping and falling.

We had to carefully *sidehill*, making our way along the side of a steep hill, parallel to the ridgeline, to reach our destination. The mother bear and her cubs were sleeping about twenty-five feet off the ground in a hollow cavity in the notch of the tree. The den was about two feet across and three feet deep.

Besides carrying food and water, we also had to lug in all the equipment necessary to extract the bear and her cubs from the tree and transport them. The biggest item we brought was a wheeled *litter*, a stretcher, that we'd need to carry the bears out on the long hike back to our vehicles.

It was fifteen degrees that day with a wind chill that drove the temperature down into the single digits. It was bitter cold. I worried that people sweating during the hike would get their clothing wet. If that happened, hypothermia could become a serious concern.

The worst part of the expedition was that we had to make several shallow stream crossings. I didn't want to have to carry waders, so I brought some heavy-duty black plastic bags to cover my boots with during the creek crossings. I didn't even think about taking my boots off to walk barefoot through the frigid streams. I didn't want to get ice between my toes.

Most of the crew didn't bring any boot coverings, though, and they didn't remove their footwear. They just splashed through the streams and hoped the water wouldn't slosh in over the tops of their boots. Some of them got wet boots and wet feet. There were a few surprised screams from the ones who got into water that was deeper than they expected.

We didn't carry any ladders with us this time. Instead, I brought a dozen of my personal screw-in tree steps to climb up to where the bears were. I used these kinds of steps to climb trees when hunting for wild hogs or other critters. Basically, they're an L-shaped four-inch length of metal with a large tapered screw on the top. You screwed them into the side of the tree, folded them down to create a little step, and hoped they'd hold your weight.

They're relatively lightweight, but can be difficult and awkward to use. As you climbed, you had to place your feet on separate steps, wrap one arm around the tree, and hold on while you screwed in another step with your free hand. Some people hated to use them. I wasn't crazy about them myself. There were much safer ways to climb a tree, but the screw-in steps were lighter and easier to carry than a ladder.

When we found the tree we were looking for, I slowly eased my way up it, screwing in one step at a time. When I got to the notch where the den was, I carefully peeked over the edge into the cavity and saw that it was full of back fur. The top of the mother bear's shoulder was only a few inches below me. I could see part of her back and one shoulder. Her head was tucked down out of sight and not exposed to the elements. She was sleeping, but wasn't totally sheltered from the rain and snow.

I cautiously climbed higher until I was above the sleeping family of bears, trying not to wake them. Bears in the Smokies are not true *hibernators*. They enter into a temporary state of deep sleep, but they can wake up if roused. I didn't want that to happen while I was up in the tree without a good escape route. I didn't want to have to jump out of a tree from that height.

When I was about six feet above the bear, I rigged a pulley and a rope. I attached a safety harness to one end. The harness was for Rick Eastridge. Rick was doing bear research for his Master's degree at the Big South Fork. He's a great guy to be around, fun-loving, humble, smart, dedicated, and hard-working. Although I installed the safety harness, I didn't merit one myself. Apparently I was expendable.

Rick and his boss, Dr. Joe Clark, loaded a pole syringe with a drug cocktail of Ketamine and Xylazine. Then they screwed a sixteen-gauge needle onto the barrel of an aluminum syringe. The plan was for Rick to climb up the tree, locate the front shoulder of the mother bear, and inject her with immobilization drugs using the jabstick.

As you might guess, when a bear gets a shot, it's not the most pleasant thing in the world, especially since we're using such a big needle. The needle we use has to be relatively large, though, so the entire 4 cc's can be given quickly.

Rick put on his harness. Then, holding the six-foot pole syringe in one hand, he slowly began to climb the trunk of the tree using the screw-in steps. A rope attached to Rick's safety harness fed through a pulley to the hands of the crew below. If he slipped, then the crew would be able to break his fall before he hit the ground.

When Rick reached the den, he looked the bear over the best he could without disturbing her, and found the place he wanted to inject. He glanced up at me and whispered, "Here we go."

One quick, solid jab and the syringe disappeared into black fur. The mother bear raised her head and snapped at Rick's face. Only a couple of feet separated his nose from her teeth. Rick climbed back down and we all waited to let the drug take effect. I stayed up in the tree above the den, with a death grip on the tree.

After fifteen minutes Rick climbed back up, this time taking a stick with him to prod her with, to make sure she was immobilized. I'd been watching the bear from my precarious perch, and hadn't seen any movement. After Rick gave her the injection she'd snuggled her head back down into the protection of the tree cavity.

I was a little concerned about the position of her head. If the bear went to sleep with her head down, her windpipe could be pinched and she might suffocate. The mother bear remained perfectly still until Rick peeked over the lip of the den opening again. She heard him this time and instantly jerked her head up and snapped her teeth right into his face, this time within inches.

That one was *close*. Obviously, she wasn't asleep. Something had gone wrong. Rick scurried back down the tree like a squirrel. I also climbed back down to the ground to see what had happened. I was especially careful to move quietly as I climbed past the mother bear.

I screwed the needle off and could see that the drugs were still in the barrel of the syringe. I tried to look through the needle but couldn't see any daylight. Then I tried to blow through it, but had no luck. When I inspected the end of the needle I could see something on it.

"What's that?" I asked Rick, tilting the needle toward him.

"Vaseline," he said.

It was standard protocol in the University of Tennessee bear research program to place some Vaseline on the end of the needle to prevent drugs from draining out of a syringe prematurely. But, on this day, with the bitter cold temperatures, the Vaseline had frozen and was clogging the needle.

The problem was easy to fix. We replaced the needle with a clean one and were ready to try again. Rick eased his way back up the tree and carefully jabbed the mother bear a second time. For a third time, she snapped at him, but he was able to avoid being bitten. We waited for the drugs to take effect, then I climbed up to check the bear. I flicked her ears and got no response. This time she was out for the count, sleeping soundly, so we could go to work.

I reached down into the den near the mother's stomach and felt three very small cubs. The mother was curled up, creating a small cavity for the tiny cubs to lie in and nurse. I asked Dr. Clark to tie a burlap bag on the end of the harness rope. I pulled it up and laid it on the mother's back. One by one, I reached in and pulled out the squalling, one-pound cubs and placed them in the bag.

As I handled each of them, their front and back legs would extend in all directions like *Garfield*. They were screaming bloody murder, too. Once they were in the bag and secure, I lowered them to the people on the ground. Leslie Morgan, the Big South Fork wildlife biologist, took them. She opened her coat and slid each of the cubs inside to keep them warm and cozy until we could get their mother down.

Rick climbed back up the tree. I was above the den and Rick below. He removed his safety harness and we lifted the mother bear enough to secure it around her. We called down to the group below and asked them to start pulling. As the rope tightened, the 125-pound mother bear slowly emerged from the cavity in the tree. Once she was clear of the tree notch, the crew carefully lowered her to the ground.

Once she was safely on the ground, the group loaded her onto the litter and started the hike back to the vehicles. Rick and I packed up all the equipment and were the last to leave the den tree. We all made it back to Parson Branch Road. Once we were on reasonably level ground, we attached a large rubber wheel to the bottom of the litter to make it easier to transport the mother bear and her cubs.

People were chitchatting and saying their feet were cold and hurting. While Rick and I had been working on the bear, the rest of the group had been waiting, standing still, and the cold temperatures had taken a toll on them, especially the ones who'd gotten their feet wet.

Most of the crew was very cold and agreed that their feet were hurting, but they were ready to start hiking again so they could warm up. Leslie, however, said her feet were numb and that she was getting nauseous. She said she'd tried to pull her boots off, but couldn't, because her shoe laces were frozen solid.

The mother bear had been asleep for about thirty minutes at this point. The group needed to keep moving so they could get her to a cage before she woke up. I told them to hike on out with the bears. Leslie, Dr. Clark, and I would be along later.

I was worried about Leslie's feet. Frostbite was a concern because it was so bitterly cold. I knew she needed some dry socks before we resumed hiking. She said he had an extra pair in her pack. I had her sit down. Dr. Clark and I looked at her boots, and sure enough, with all the ice and snow packed around them, we could barely see her laces. We had to beat and bang on her shoes to break the ice off of them, but finally we were able loosen the laces, and pull her boots off.

Leslie replaced the cold wet socks with warm dry ones, and started feeling better. Soon she was able to continue the hike back to the truck. By the time we rejoined the others, Rick had already put the bear family into a transfer cage. The mother bear was starting to wake up and we could hear the surprisingly loud and distinctive purr coming from the babies as they nursed.

We were out in the cold about seven hours that day. It was a very tough day and a potentially dangerous one to be in the backcountry, but sometimes that's just part of the job.

The next day, we placed the mother and cubs in a ground den at the Big South Fork. We drugged her and placed her in the den first. Then, the cubs came next. Before we placed the cubs in with their mother, Dr. Clark smeared Vaseline on their backs and the tops of their heads, so when the mother woke, she'd lick the Vaseline off to clean them. That would help remove the human smell. This time, the Vaseline worked well.

In the spring, Leslie told us that she'd tracked the mother and cubs moving about. Fortunately, the family group accepted their new home and stayed there. Mission accomplished.

ON THE ROAD AGAIN
WITH TRAVELLER

SOME CRITTERS require more help than others. A few animals require a spectacular amount of attention. But, when it's a species that had been totally wiped out in the Park and that we were hoping to bring back, I always tried to go the extra mile—or in a few cases, hundreds of extra miles on foot, in ATV's, cars, trucks, trailers, and even airplanes. This was especially true for our efforts to return elk to the Smokies.

We decided to start our elk reintroduction program in the beautiful, isolated Cataloochee Valley of North Carolina. Cataloochee is a hard drive of eighty miles from Park Headquarters, some of it along steep, curvy, narrow, unpaved mountain roads with no guardrails. I've made the drive countless times. I've made it in all seasons, in every kind of weather, in daylight and dark.

I made the trip an unbelievable number of times for one special case: a bull elk we designated as Elk #22. He was the 22nd elk we captured at Land Between the Lakes, Tennessee in the spring of 2001 and moved to the Cataloochee Valley.

Elk #22 and two of the other bull elk apparently weren't happy in Cataloochee and decided to take a walk and look for greener pastures. They left in the early summer of their first year in the valley and roamed down the Pigeon River, leaving the protection of the Park. We located them over in Waterville, North Carolina, near the Tennessee-North Carolina state line along I-40. We knew they went there because we had radio collars on them.

Two of the bulls didn't like what they saw and turned back, but Elk #22 continued to Tennessee to the Hartford exit on I-40. He stayed in the general area for a while but was seen switching sides of the Interstate for a couple of weeks. Eventually he continued his exploratory travels and ended up on a small farm in Cocke County near Newport, Tennessee. He was now about twenty miles, as the crow flies, from Cataloochee.

Because the elk was outside the boundary of the National Park, we didn't have jurisdiction over him. I called the Tennessee Wildlife Resources Agency to ask how they wanted the situation handled. I offered to go capture the elk and bring him back to Cataloochee.

Bob Nichols, who was the Regional Area Manager for Tennessee Wildlife Resources Agency and a good friend of mine, responded to my question by teasing me. "Let's wait and see what he does," he said. "If he stays out of trouble, he's a State of Tennessee elk and you can leave him where he is, but if he causes a problem, he's a federal elk and you need to come get him and take him back!" Then he laughed.

"Let's leave him for now," Bob said, more serious this time, "Maybe he'll go back to Cataloochee on his own for the upcoming rut."

That sounded fair to me. I didn't want to have to move him unless it was absolutely necessary. We're not working with squirrels or rabbits here. It's not pleasant to try and capture a 700-pound wild animal and do the heavy labor that's necessary to move him around while he's unconscious. Seven hundred pounds is a huge animal. It's like handling a giant sack of potatoes. There aren't any handles.

Later that fall, in October, Elk #22 did what we hoped he'd do. He pulled up stakes, broke camp on the farm in Newport, Tennessee, and started traveling back to Cataloochee, North Carolina. Unfortunately, on his return, he came extremely close to causing a major wreck on I-40 at mile marker 4 near one of the tunnels.

A National Park Service employee, former University of Tennessee classmate, and good friend of mine, Janice Pelton, called Dispatch to say she was at mile marker 4 on I-40 and was watching Elk #22. He was standing beside the Interstate hoping to cross and get back on the same side of the Interstate as Cataloochee. This was a very dangerous situation for the elk and for the people driving on the Interstate. The traffic in that area is extremely heavy. Janice said that eighteen-wheelers were locking up their brakes to avoid hitting the elk. This was a recipe for disaster.

Soon afterwards, Janice called again to say that the elk had run up into the woods on the east side of the Interstate and had gone out of sight. I needed help so I called Brandon Wear, our elk field person, and told him I'd meet him at his office in Big Creek. When I arrived, Brandon jumped into my vehicle and we took off to try to find our wayward, wandering elk.

Using radio telemetry signals from the elk's collar, we could tell he was traveling at a steady pace on the east side of, and parallel to, the Interstate. We knew he was looking for a place to cross, but there's nothing except cliffs along that stretch of the Interstate. We couldn't get eyes on the elk, because he was in the thick, brushy woods. Then it started to get dark.

At that time of day, eighteen wheelers fly through this area. It's a mountainous section of the Tennessee-North Carolina state line that we call *The Gorge*. The big trucks are normally bumper to bumper winding through a long series of sharp curves. They're traveling so close together that they remind me of a freight train barreling down a railroad track.

To make things worse, there's a five-foot concrete barrier in the median. The wall and the heavy traffic of semis and other vehicles made the chances of any animal successfully crossing the Interstate highly unlikely. Most of the animals attempting to cross would be injured or killed.

I was very concerned that Elk #22 would try to cross after it got dark and cause a terrible wreck. But there was nothing we could do, so Brandon and I went home for the night. All we could do was hope and pray that no one got hurt before we could find the big elk and get him away from the Interstate.

I didn't sleep very well that night. I kept expecting the phone to ring and to be Dispatch reporting that an elk had caused a pileup on I-40. Luckily, that didn't happen. Brandon went back the next morning to try to find Elk #22 with his telemetry equipment. He drove to the last place we'd located him, near Exit #7, Harmon Den.

He pulled out his antenna and started listening for a signal on the east side of the Interstate, but he didn't hear anything. *Where did the elk go?*

Brandon then turned his antenna in the opposite direction and heard a strong *beep...beep...beep.*

That was great news. Apparently, sometime during the night, the elk had travelled through the overpass at Harmon Den. By doing this, he'd avoided the five-foot concrete abutment, otherwise known as the *Wall of Death*. Then he'd crossed the Little Pigeon River and finally gotten away from the interstate. Now he was headed cross-country and in the right direction—toward the Park.

We were happy to discover that Elk #22 was now on the same side of the road as Cataloochee and we hoped he was on his way back to the main herd.

The next day he arrived back in Cataloochee as we'd hoped. He'd made it back on his own! We were extremely relieved and hoped he'd never leave again. But, of course, that was wishful thinking.

Elk #22 was a young bull, only about three or four years old. He probably left the area in the first place because he got banged up a few times by the bigger, more dominant bulls. Bull #1 was the herd bull then and Elk #22 was much smaller and a long way from being able to compete for females during the breeding season.

After a couple of weeks in Cataloochee, Elk #22 took off again and went back to Newport, Tennessee to the same farm he'd visited during the summer. I assumed he'd found himself a new home. I should've known better. If I'd learned one thing working with wild animals, it was to never assume *anything*!

Then one morning Brandon called and said he couldn't pick up Elk #22's signal. He asked for permission to try to find the animal from the air. I told him to go ahead.

He managed to locate the signal from Elk #22 in an area northeast of the Park in Greene County, Tennessee, near the Nolichucky River. Once the general area was identified, Brandon could resume his search on the ground to pinpoint Elk #22's hangout. But before he had a chance to drive to Greene County to try to get a specific location, I got several calls from residents in the area.

People were mostly okay with an elk being there. They were just reporting the sighting of an elk wearing a radio collar and ear tags. I talked with a farmer who owned a fairly large cattle operation where Elk #22 was staying. I asked if he wanted us to come and move him. He said the elk wasn't causing any problems. He graciously told to me to not worry about the elk, that it was okay.

I'd been in this situation before, though, when someone said the elk was fine. In a few days the scenario would change and the landowner would want the animal removed. Elk can cause problems for farmers. This is the reason we don't put elk in areas with a lot of active farming.

I asked Brandon to drive up to Greene County and locate our wandering elk. Fortunately he was able to find him. By this time the critter had gotten the nickname *Traveller*. But before Jennifer Murrow and I could get there, Traveller had already knocked down a fence and spooked some of the farmer's cows. Jennifer pinpointed his position with her receiver in a big thicket on the side of a hill. We chose a stakeout spot where we could observe his movements, and tried to make a plan to dart him and get him back home.

Traveller was running the bovine bulls away from their feed. He'd let the female cattle eat with him, but not the males. The farmer asked me in a polite way to get him out of there, and emphasized I shouldn't drag my feet about it.

Traveller knew what Park Service vehicles looked like by this time and was very wary around them. We'd darted and handled him so much that he was leery of rangers, too, particularly me!

Dusk was approaching. I saw him emerge from the thicket and start walking down the hill toward where we sat. He wanted to cross the road and go into another field that had cattle feeders in it.

I suspected this was his routine, to bed down all day in the thicket, and then just before dark, travel over to the feeders and have supper. I watched the elk trot down the hill.

We were scrambling around trying to get the dart and gun loaded. I told Jennifer that I needed her to get a measurement of the distance from me to the animal. As we approached the place where the elk was going to cross the road, Jennifer was hanging out the window of the truck with the rangefinder.

"What's the distance?" I asked, as I got my dart rifle ready. I was waiting for Traveller to jump a fence and walk across the middle of the road so I could get a clear shot. I was praying that no other vehicles would happen to drive down the road toward us.

"Jennifer, what's the distance?" I asked again.

I heard her push the button on the rangefinder. "Thirty-five yards," she said.

The elk jumped the fence as I dialed in my power setting for thirty-five yards. I quickly rested the crosshairs on the elk's hip, and squeezed the trigger. The dart hit and we saw the flash indicating that the charge had detonated. Jennifer and I smiled and high-fived each other. Locating and catching a wild elk in a strange area can be very difficult. I think I might've had a little divine help that time. I needed it and was grateful for it.

When Traveller went down and was safely asleep, several of the local farmers and neighbors came over to watch the goings on. Everyone wanted to get their picture made with him. Then they helped me saw off his antlers as the Canadian experts recommended we do when an elk's rack got to a significant size. We did this so we could fit him into a narrow trailer designed to hold cattle.

Removing the hard-boned antlers was not at all painful for him but he'd look a little less manly until he started growing new ones next April. After his antlers were removed, the group offered to help me load him.

When he was loaded into the trailer I gave him the reversal drug because I needed him to stand up. So I waited and helped stabilize him as he got back on his feet. Then we took off back to North Carolina. Traveller had ridden in a trailer several times at this point. I guess he was getting used to it by now.

Since he wasn't old enough or tough enough to compete for females in Cataloochee, I needed to look elsewhere for a place to take him. He'd made the rounds throughout the valley and there were just too many bull elk there that were much bigger and more dominant than him. He needed a fresh start somewhere and I decided that place was Oconaluftee, near Cherokee, North Carolina. There were only seven elk there. I figured he'd have a better chance to make it there because it was a less aggressive environment.

We took him up Big Cove Road to a place above the site of the new Cherokee school. There were a few elk standing around in the field when we got there. Of course all the bulls had antlers, except Traveller. When I saw that, I got worried.

In hindsight I wished we hadn't sawed off his antlers. We did it to keep him from getting hurt during transport, but it presented a problem for him when we arrived at our destination.

I was right to worry. When I opened the trailer door, Traveller wouldn't come out. We waited and waited, and then finally we had to push him out. He shuffled away looking pitiful. He had his head down as he walked slowly away from the trailer.

His walk and his body posture said, *I'm a failure in life.* The two other bulls thought the same thing and came running toward him. They acted as if they wanted to fight, but he didn't have antlers to fight back with. He just walked off with a mopey, sad look. He'd been bullied, literally. The other bulls had little sympathy for him. He was the new kid on the block and they wanted to make sure he knew who was in charge around there. I felt really bad for Traveller.

Then something interesting happened.

All five of the female elk came over to him, apparently trying to console him after the bulls ran him off. It was fun to watch. They clustered around him and nudged him gently. They walked along beside him and stayed with him.

When Traveller got all the women around him, it sure caught the attention of the bulls. I wondered what the cows were saying to Traveller and what the bulls were thinking. Traveler and the female elk walked slowly into a thicket together and soon were out of sight.

If Traveller could say anything to the other bulls, I imagined it might've been something like, *Who's laughing now, big boys?*

I assumed he'd leave the area again this time, too, but he didn't. With his long history of moving out of the Park, we'd decided that if he left again, we might have to put him down for good. He was becoming a safety risk, but I didn't want to think about that yet. I wanted to stay positive and hoped he'd settle down. That was more wishful thinking on my part.

Traveller stayed in Oconaluftee all winter and into the next summer. His antlers started growing back and this time he had something to display to his companions—a large six-by-six rack, six points on each side. Finally, he might be king of the hill for a change.

I was pleased and Traveller must've been, too, because he stayed in Oconaluftee for a couple of years after that. Then one day, for no obvious reason, he took off during the summer to a small community northeast of Bryson City, called Ela, pronounced *EE-la*.

A man called to tell me Traveller was hanging around his farm. He said the elk wasn't causing any problems. He just wanted me to know where he was. I told him I appreciated his call and asked him to let me know if there was any change.

Well, of course things changed. It didn't take very long for Traveller to get in trouble again. When I got to work one morning, I had a call on my voicemail from the farmer.

Traveller was still at the same farm, but now he'd started playing with the large round bales of hay, shoving them around like toys. When hay is round-baled, it's rolled up like roll of tape. Traveller was unrolling the bales. That wasn't good. It might've been fun for the elk, but it wasn't amusing for the farmer.

The round bales weighed over 1,000 pounds apiece. That was more than the elk weighed, but it was something he could shove around pretty easily. He was pushing the bales all over the field, rolling them onto fences or into the creek, moving them around like they weighed nothing. The farmer wasn't happy. Neither was I.

Steven Dobey, who'd replaced Brandon Wear as the elk person on our wildlife crew and was now Jennifer Murrow's husband, went with me to dart Traveller. When we drove over to Ela, Steven had already pinpointed the elk's exact location.

When we got there, we mapped out a plan. Steven showed me a field the elk normally fed in just before dark. We had two or three hours before dark, so, knowing it could be a late night, we drove down to the local store to get a bite to eat. While we were there, we saw a news alert on their small television saying Michael Jackson had died.

I turned to an older gentlemen who was wearing bib overalls and chewing tobacco, and said, "Can you believe Michael Jackson has died?"

"No," the gentleman said. Then he asked, "Who the heck's Michael Jackson?"

We drove back to the field and pulled out our equipment, preparing for the big bull to show his face. Sure enough, Traveller popped out into the field just as Steven had predicted. I worked my way along the creek and positioned myself in an area near where the elk would browse. As soon as Traveller was within range, I fired the dart gun and the dart found its mark. He moved off a short distance, lay down, and was soon asleep.

We loaded him into the horse trailer, gave him the reversal drugs to wake him up, and waited. After he hopped up, we hauled him back to Cataloochee again, thinking that surely he was big enough *now* to compete for the ladies in the valley. His tall rack was impressive. He looked like he was wearing *big boy* pants now, but we'd have to see what the other Cataloochee elk thought.

We released him and this time I thought he was home to stay. But he wasn't. He didn't stay. I couldn't believe it!

He left Cataloochee again and walked all the way back to his old stomping grounds near Newport. It was spring when I drove over to the area. I had to talk to a lot of people to find Traveller. I went up to a house near where I thought he might be and knocked on the front door. An elderly lady opened it and I asked her if she'd seen an elk running around. She said the last time he'd been seen that she knew of, he was on a horse farm over the ridge from her place.

She was happy to chat about the elk. "Wait a minute, sir," she said. "I wanna show you somethin." She came back to the door carrying a photo of an elk. "Is this the elk you're lookin for?" she asked.

"Yes ma'am," I said, "it is. He's older now and bigger."

She'd taken a picture of Traveller in her back yard, the first time he'd visited the area five years earlier. She said Traveller wasn't a problem and I could just leave him there forever. She pointed me in the right direction, though, and I went over to a farm where they raised miniature ponies. Traveller was there. The little ponies were so small they could walk back and forth under his belly.

It was early evening and time for him to start feeding. At about 7 p.m., here he came, easing his way out into the field. I waited until he walked down a fencerow and jumped into another pasture. Then he was close enough for a shot. I drove up as close to him as possible and darted him. After being darted so many times, you'd think he'd realize who we were and what we were up to, but by this time he was almost tame.

When the dart hit him, he ran away from us and into the backyard of a nearby house and went to sleep there. A crowd of local people came to see him. We covered his eyes so he wouldn't be frightened and let people touch him and get their photos taken with him.

Everyone was excited and they kept asking, "Do you have to take him away?"

I assured them that moving him was the safest thing for everyone. Then we wrestled him into the trailer, went through the drug reversal procedure, helped him up onto his hooves, and took him back to Oconaluftee for his second release there.

I was about to run out of options for Traveller. I'd moved him to Oconaluftee twice and Cataloochee twice. I hoped this would be the last time I had to move him. He stayed in the Oconaluftee area for a while. Unfortunately he was accepting food from residents and visitors.

There were enough people willing to offer him food that he became very tame and food-conditioned. The big bull was becoming a safety risk. The future for Traveller at this point didn't look very bright.

He'd hang out with domestic cows or horses. He'd walk up into people's carports and eat in their yards. I think he would've eaten out of your hand if given the opportunity. He'd been fed a lot by this point, which meant he'd become a potentially dangerous animal.

Unfortunately, he now had no fear of people and sooner or later was going to hurt someone, either accidentally or on purpose. He might seem rather tame most of the year, but during the rut season he'd be very unpredictable and aggressive. He was a huge wild animal with a big rack. He was the king of the hill these days, but he faced new battles now of a type he'd never encountered before.

His lack of fear of people couldn't be allowed to continue. I knew this food-conditioned behavior wasn't exactly his fault. He was a wild animal just trying to make a living. But still, the safety risks were the same. If he hurt someone, especially a child, it would be tragic.

It was now summer. Traveller's antlers were growing and still in the velvet stage. He'd moved from Oconaluftee over the ridge to an area called Cooper's Creek that was under the jurisdiction of the Eastern Band of the Cherokee Indians. In this area, the Cherokee people have property where tribal members can plant gardens. Traveller had homed in on these gardens and was damaging the food that people worked hard to grow.

For many people, these gardens provided food they needed throughout the year. I discussed the situation with Mike Carraway from the North Carolina Wildlife Resources Commission and Forrest Parker from the Eastern Band of the Cherokees. We talked about what we should do with Traveller. Together we decided that the best thing for human safety, property protection, and for the overall success of the elk reintroduction program, was to put Traveller down before something terrible happened. Even though the decision was the right one, I was sick about it.

Traveller was on Cooper's Creek in the Cherokee gardens when a member of the Cherokee Tribe went over and shot and killed him. I was there when it happened. Now I had to move the big fellow one last time, but this time it was in the back of our *Boar* pickup truck. I hauled his body back over the mountain to a place near Elkmont. We collected some necessary samples from him for disease testing, then we buried Traveller.

It was a sad situation. I'd put a tremendous amount of time and energy and money into trying to keep Traveller wild and inside the Park, but my best efforts weren't enough to accomplish that. I'd hauled him out of Newport and Greene County, Tennessee, and Ela, North Carolina. But I couldn't keep him safe and away from people.

Thank heavens I didn't have to be the one to shoot him. That would've been tough.

Although Traveller was a wanderer, most of the fault for his death lies with the people who fed him. I wish they'd thought about the consequences of feeding him before they did it. But, as I've seen over and over, some people just don't care.

Traveller and I had a long history together. I'd spent more time with him than any other animal in the Smokies. It had been ten years since I first saw him standing in a field at Land Between the Lakes. As I covered him in his grave, I remembered the first time I'd ever laid eyes on him.

I'd said to Dr. Ed Ramsay, "Now's there's a good one!" And he was.

THIRD TIME'S A CHARM

WE THINK NATURE TAKES CARE of wild animals so they'll know everything they need to know by pure instinct. But that's not true. Animals *don't* always know everything they need to know. Just like us, there are many things they have to learn, and some of those lessons are painful, or even fatal.

Whether you're talking about animals or people, some mothers are just better than others at protecting their young. There are lots of predators in the Park and they're always on the lookout for young animals because they're easier targets. Newborns are in significant jeopardy during the first weeks of their lives when they're not very mobile.

Healthy populations of large predators, like bears, bobcats, or coyotes, serve a good purpose by keeping the number of animals like deer and elk in check. However, large numbers of predators concentrated in an area can make it tough to bring back a species we've lost, like elk.

Bears in the Smokies are very efficient predators. Some of them are clever enough to walk grid patterns in the open fields searching for newborns and baby animals that might be hidden in the grass. They've learned over the years when it's time for deer and elk to drop their fawns and calves and they take advantage of the easy food source. To a hungry bear, an elk calf is similar to a deer.

The first group of elk we released in the Park came from Land Between the Lakes in western Kentucky near the Tennessee border, and the next group was from Elk Island National Park in Canada. Neither of those places had black bears or any other predators that preyed heavily on elk, so the animals we got were very naïve about bears and what they were capable of doing. Unfortunately our elk had to learn the hard way how to protect themselves and their young.

Elk Cow #15 was a great example of the learning process. She was the 15th elk that I captured at Land Between the Lakes during the winter of 2000. She was already pregnant when she was first released in Cataloochee. A few of the elk had calves that first year, but none of them was ready to deal with an experienced population of predators that was just waiting for the calving period to start.

Bears in the Cataloochee area were already primed for the deer fawns to be born around mid-May, and now the elk would be calving at approximately the same time. For a bear, catching and killing a baby elk calf would be easy.

The first year, Elk #15 lost her calf. It died the same day it was born because bears killed it in a field in Cataloochee. Several Park visitors saw it happen. Elk #15 was watching, too. A bear grabbed the baby elk and killed it with one quick shake. Then the bear walked out of the field with the calf and disappeared into the woods.

The mother elk ran up and down the field for a long time afterwards, not knowing what to do. She was making a loud sound called a *bark*, a noise that alerts the other elk to danger. She did it over and over again. Nothing like this had ever happened to her before.

We were all upset about it, but that sort of thing happens in the wild. I wished the bears could've waited until the elk population was larger before they started to prey on them, but they didn't. Survival in the wild isn't easy. It's survival of the fittest. For the elk to make it in the Smokies, they'd have to learn how to coexist with bears.

The second year, Elk #15 became pregnant again. This time, when it was time for her to calve, she moved a couple of miles away from the Cataloochee meadows. Because she was wearing a radio collar we knew where she was. We were going to hike in to see if we could find her calf so we could put a little collar on it, too. But just as the crew was mobilizing to walk in to search for the newborn, the mother elk returned to the main herd, with no calf.

We don't know exactly what happened to her baby. All we know is that the mother came back to the herd without a newborn. She was no longer pregnant and no calf was ever seen with her. We can only assume a bear, coyote, or bobcat got it. Whatever happened, it would be a full year before she could try again.

Deer and elk, *cervids*, are graced with a natural survival trait that helps protect their offspring. Newborn deer fawns and elk calves have very little smell, so when the mother moves away from the herd to give birth, it's harder for predators to find the virtually odorless babies. But even with this protection, bears and other predators know when calving is going on and the smell of blood from the birthing process allows them to home in on the newborns.

Immediately after the calf is born, many of the mothers eat the afterbirth, the *placenta*, to lessen the chances for detection by predators. Then they move the calf away from the birth site, hide it in thick vegetation, and walk away. The scentless calf, lies perfectly still until the mother returns, so a hungry predator can walk very, very close to the baby and pass it by without even realizing the calf is there.

During feeding time, the mother calls for the newborn to come over and nurse. Then, after it eats, the wobbly little elk ambles back to its hiding place to wait for its next meal. Many newborns make it through this precarious time, but not all.

It was nearly two and a half years after Elk #15 arrived at her new home in Cataloochee when it was time for her third calf to be born. The elk researchers kept a close watch on her visually, and by means of her collar. People say that *the third time's a charm*. We hoped that would prove to be true for this mother.

Elk researcher Jennifer Murrow called one morning to let me know that Elk #15 was missing. They couldn't pick up a signal from her collar. Jennifer said she'd start looking outside the Cataloochee Valley to see if they could find her.

The next morning I was being interviewed on the Sugarlands Nature Trail by a film crew from Atlanta as part of a program that would air on TBS. During the interview, I overheard a maintenance employee, Tom Rickman, calling Park Dispatch on the radio. Tom said he was on the Balsam Mountain Road, a two-lane North Carolina road that runs from the Blue Ridge Parkway to Balsam Mountain Campground at around 5,000' in elevation.

"There's an elk cow over here that's staggerin down the road," Tom said, "and there's two coyotes runnin right behind her."

I wondered what in the world was wrong with the elk. Had the coyotes chased her and caused her to fall and injure herself? Had they grabbed her from behind and damaged her back legs, hamstringing her? As I wondered what might be going on, I thought to myself, *a staggering elk cow with coyotes chasing her during calving time.* Then I said out loud, "Oh crap, she's having her calf!"

The startled television interviewer said, "Who's having a calf?"

"The elk cow," I said, "and the coyotes are after her."

Apparently the elk cow's water had broken and the coyotes picked up the scent of blood and fluids. The cow was probably in the process of giving birth and as the calf was moving through the birth canal it was causing partial paralysis of her back legs. That was why she was staggering.

The interview was instantly over. I had to leave and head to Balsam Mountain.

Before we pulled out of the parking lot just above Park Headquarters, I heard the Tom Rickman talking to Dispatch again, "700, the elk has dropped a baby elk calf on the side of the road."

I grabbed the radio, and said, "Tom, are the coyotes still around?"

"I don't see any," he said.

"Can you please stand next to the calf until I get there?" I asked.

"Will do," he said, "and Kim, there's an elk nearby. Her ear tag is #15.

I wondered to myself, *#15?*

I quickly scanned a map and realized that she was about seven miles from Cataloochee. After losing her calf in the Cataloochee Valley for two years in a row, this time she'd traveled seven miles and climbed into a high elevation area to have her baby. This mamma elk was becoming wiser.

On the way over to Balsam Mountain, I tried to contact Jennifer several times on both the radio and phone, but couldn't reach her. I called Dispatch and asked them to keep trying. Finally, I got her on the radio and told her to bring the calf collaring equipment over to the Balsam Mountain area because Elk #15 had dropped her calf.

"10-4," she said, "I'm on my way."

I could hear the excitement in her voice. We both felt so sorry for this mother who'd lost her first two calves. We wanted to do every-thing we could to help this one survive.

Wild animals are programmed to reproduce. It's part of the sur-vival process to maintain their species. In humans, losing a newborn baby or a young child has to be one of the toughest things to ever have to deal with, especially for the mother. I assume animals don't relate to the loss of their newborns in the same way as humans, but still, it must be rough for a mother in the wild to lose her offspring, especially soon after it's born.

We all arrived at about the same time and met where Tom was parked. He pointed to the newborn and said the calf's mother was across the road in the trees. Jennifer went to the little elk and placed a small blindfold over its eyes to help it stay calm. Then she quickly put a little collar on it.

When we were finished and Jennifer and her crew had packed everything up, we carried the newborn away from the road and placed it in an area with thicker vegetation to hide it better. As I was settling the small calf on the ground, its blindfold slipped off. The calf looked up and began to cry out in a loud voice. I assume he was saying, *Help me, Mommy*, because Elk #15 came crashing down the steep bank, galloped across the road, and charged directly toward me.

Jennifer was only a few feet away and without hesitation jumped in to save the day. She leaped between me and the charging elk, raising her hand like a traffic cop. She screamed, "Stop!"

When Jennifer shouted, the mother elk locked on the brakes and slid to a stop. She stood there, staring at Jennifer.

I'd been saved by a woman, and that was fine by me. The fact that Jennifer was a *take charge* kind of person was evident that day. As for me, when the elk charged, I was ready to let go of the calf and get the heck outta there. But now, with Jennifer standing between me and the mother, I took my time and gently bedded the calf down in a comfortable concealed location.

After we moved away, the cow eased over to her calf and nudged it with her nose. As the mother tended to her baby, she kept glancing down the road in our direction. I think she was keeping an eye on Jennifer. I believe Jennifer intimidated the elk. I know she scared me.

But I sure was thankful she was there. Most people would've run, including me, but not Jennifer. Nothing and no one was gonna push her around. I thanked her and gave her a hug.

She was my hero.

A few weeks passed and Elk #15 remained in the higher altitude area where she'd given birth. It looked like she was finally going to succeed in raising her first calf in the Smokies, and we were happy for her.

Then one morning Jennifer called, crying and upset, saying that Elk #15 was back in Cataloochee grazing in the meadows with the other elk, and she'd left her baby calf seven miles away on top of the mountain, *alone*.

We were crushed. They'd been together for a while now, and this wasn't supposed to happen. Was Elk #15 a bad mother? Had she deserted her baby and left it to die?

"Can we go get it and take it to Cataloochee?" Jennifer asked.

"Jennifer, we can't make the mother accept the calf if she doesn't want it," I said. "Let's wait until morning and see if anything changes before we decide what to do."

Jennifer agreed, but I could tell her heart wasn't in it.

It was a restless night for everyone. The next morning at dawn Jennifer was in the Cataloochee Valley. She dialed her receiver to the frequency of Elk #15 and confirmed that she was somewhere close by. Then she switched to the frequency of the newborn calf's collar, and as soon as she did, a loud *beep-beep-beep* rang out.

Such a strong signal startled her. She thought, *That's way too strong to be coming from seven miles away.* Then she realized, *The calf's here in the valley, too*!

Jennifer drove along the road until she saw a group of elk in the field above the Ranger Station. She pulled out her binoculars and looked at ear tag numbers. Elk #15 was standing on the edge of the group, and right beside her was a baby calf, alive and well.

Jennifer called me on the radio to give me the news. I was extremely happy to hear it.

Although Elk #15 had lost her first two calves, she was able to learn from her bad experiences. And even though at first it looked like she'd deserted her third calf, something had happened during the night. She'd walked the seven miles back up the mountain and returned to her calf.

She'd then led the baby elk through the thickets, up and down the steep hills and hollers, cross-country in the dark, back to the valley. Since she'd first left Cataloochee when she was pregnant, she'd walked at least twenty-eight miles to deliver her baby and raise her calf safely. She'd made a fourteen-mile round-trip, by herself in a single night, just to make sure the coast was clear. Now both mother and baby were safely back in Cataloochee with the main herd.

In the following years, every May, Elk #15 repeated her seven-mile trek up the mountain to calve. She also led her offspring to this same area when they were old enough to have calves of their own. She'd learned an important lesson and now she was passing it along to help other elk raise their own young in the wilds of the Smokies.

Nowadays, a small heard of elk resides for much of the year in the high elevations of Balsam Mountain and I know which elk was responsible for them being there.

THE BEST DAY OF MY CAREER

IT'S EASY TO REMEMBER the best day of my career. It was the first day I saw a herd of elk roaming free in the fields of Cataloochee Valley. Cataloochee is a special place. Like Cades Cove, the isolated valley has been maintained by the Park to look similar to the way it did generations ago.

I was on my way over to Cataloochee to meet with the area ranger, Walt West. As I drove, I thought about the previous years of effort and the long grueling government compliance process to acquire and release the elk.

It had been brutal for me and the others who worked on the reintroduction program. *Nothing is easy*, I thought. Returning elk to the nation's most visited National Park had been a challenge, to say the least.

On my way over the mountain, I called Walt on the radio to discuss a rendezvous location. He told me he was in the large open fields in the floor of the valley and suggested I meet him there. Even though I was driving through one of the most spectacularly beautiful landscapes on earth, my mind was still in racing, worrying about setting up the necessary agreements with the state of North Carolina and the Cherokee Tribe, schedules, time sheets, training programs, and other endless government paperwork.

As I drove around the last curve, suddenly a panorama of the valley opened up, and I could see half a dozen cars parked alongside the road. People were standing at the edge of the field looking at something through their binoculars. As I got closer, I could see there were a dozen elk grazing in one of the meadows. I pulled my Explorer off the road and got out.

I stared at the small herd of elk, unable to speak. The sight gave me goosebumps. All I could think was, *Wow, will you look at that?*

Walt came over to where I was standing, and said, "It's pretty neat, isn't it?"

"Yeah," I said. "Seeing them like this makes it all worthwhile."

I'd finally taken the time to stop and smell the roses.

For years I'd heard so many pessimistic people predict failure for the elk program, "It'll never happen," they said.

Well, it *had* happened. Elk were once again living in the Great Smoky Mountains National Park.

We'd made history.

People love to see large wild animals, like elk and bears. The *charismatic megafauna,* as scientists refer to them, are a symbol of wildness. They're majestic beasts that are mysterious, potentially dangerous, and definitely unpredictable. Some people are so mesmerized when they see big creatures, they lose their sense of reality. Some of them don't know any better than to try to walk up to a wild animal.

But there are other visitors who are well aware of the Park's rules about not willfully approaching bears or elk closer than fifty yards. They know you're not supposed to get close enough to disturb any wild animal, or interrupt whatever they're doing. Nevertheless some of these people just don't care. They're willing to close the distance and try to get a better photograph, or to pet them, or even feed them.

I suspect some people might be trying to make a statement about how brave, or foolhardy, they are by walking up close to a bear or elk. I guess they hope to impress other people, but many of them are a long way from being a Daniel Boone, Davy Crockett, or John Wayne. To me, they're more along the lines of Pee Wee Herman.

I think some people forget that, here in the Smokies, we're only visitors to the homes of the critters. Because of our presence, some wild animals may suffer, other times they may benefit. It's a difficult balancing act to see if we can all peacefully coexist in this little bit of heaven called the Smoky Mountains.

In trying to protect the Smokies wildlife and their home, sometimes the animals need our help. I've seen visitors chase wild animals, but I've also seen wild animals chase people. Over the years, there have been several instances where an elk chased me or someone else. But the one of the best moments happened in Oconaluftee, near the town of Cherokee, North Carolina.

There are open fields on both sides of the four-lane road in this area where it's common for a small group of elk to feed during the early mornings and late evenings.

On this particular evening, the elk were grouped in several clusters on both sides of the road. For a while, some of them were even standing *in* the road. Eventually though, they wandered across the highway to graze together out in the middle of a field.

There was an impressive-looking bull elk about 200 yards from the road. He was too far away for me to read his ear tag, but I knew it would identify him as Elk #3. That particular bull elk was unmistakable on account of his huge rack. He had a very impressive display of antlers.

He'd had been the very first elk to leave Cataloochee and make his way over to Luftee. Since then, he'd made several trips back and forth, and apparently he'd spilled the beans about this new paradise on the other side of the mountain because other elk had followed him to the area.

The elk were feeding as normally as possible with so many visitors watching them. Then some tourists decided to leave their vehicles to get a closer look. They set out walking across the open field toward the herd.

The stalkers were heading straight for Elk #3. When other visitors noticed this, they decided to join the party. People usually know they shouldn't approach a wild animal, but there's always one in every crowd who has to do it. And if one person moves closer, others will follow suit, and pretty soon it's a mob scene. On this particular day, there were about thirty or forty people slowly walking toward Elk #3.

The stalkers are often assisted by a few guilty souls who keep watch on the road and will call out if they see a ranger drive up. On this day, no rangers or volunteers were around to chase the people away from the elk. This time, Elk #3 and the others were on their own in dealing with the approaching crowd.

Elk #3 is a big bull. He's fairly tolerant of visitors for most of the year, but not so much during the breeding season. During his travels, people had fed him to the point that he'd lost a lot of his fear of them. When he was young, he'd run away if people approached. Now, he'd let them come closer, but he still had his limits.

The crowd of tourists made a semi-circle and managed to get to within about fifteen yards of the 800-pound bull. Some of the people with small children tried to get even closer, snapping their cameras every step of the way. Elk #3 was becoming agitated by the group of gawkers.

He stopped grazing and stared at them. They stared back. Apparently they'd crossed the line and he was getting ready to take charge of the situation. This time it wasn't going to be necessary for a ranger or anyone else to save the elk from the tourists. This elk could save himself. He was about to educate some visitors about the consequences of approaching a wild animal.

Elk #3 started slowly ambling toward the people, and it began to dawn on the tourists that maybe they were too close, so they slowly moved back, in the general direction of their cars. Then the bull picked up his pace a bit and the people did the same. When they got about half way back to their cars, some of the visitors spun around and began a quick march across the wide grassy expanse.

Elk #3 broke into a trot. The tourists broke into a trot as well.

Then the elk started galloping toward the fleeing crowd. It was like a bomb had exploded in the middle of the group. People went wild. They were screaming, dragging their kids, sprinting across a couple hundred yards of open ground toward any protection they could find. People were tripping and falling. Cameras, daypacks, hats, and sunglasses were flying in all directions.

Both elk and tourists were running wide open. People were racing in every direction. The fastest runners made it back to the cars first and were tossing their children inside and slamming the doors. Then the ignitions roared to life and they quickly sped away.

Elk #3 could've hurt someone in the fleeing crowd, but he didn't. I'd always wondered what happened when no rangers were around. Now I knew, and I had to laugh.

The big bull elk administered a very effective and memorable lesson as to why no one should ever approach animals in the wild. All the employees in the Park put together couldn't have done a better job.

Elk #3 shook his head at the last of the stragglers and then stretched his neck out and bugled a long, eerie, scream that filled the air. By the time the sound quit bouncing and echoing off the walls of the surrounding mountains, there was no sign of the crowd.

Elk #3 returned to his evening feeding session, as did the rest of the small herd. I'm not sure if elk smile or not, but if they do, I'd guess that Elk #3 had a little smile on his face that evening.

I know I did.

The wilderness was *home* to these creatures, and human beings were intruding. This encroachment meant we had a responsibility to lend a helping hand, if necessary. But it was comforting to know that, in some situations, the wild creatures could do just fine on their own.

As I turned to leave the valley, I smiled to myself as I thought, *It's just another day in the Park.*

APPENDIX: ENCOUNTERING BLACK BEARS IN THE SMOKIES

Bears are a lot like people. Each one has a different personality, and every day brings new situations that affect their mood. Bears will act differently when they're hungry, scared, or upset, in the same way people will be more short-tempered if they're on a diet or if they're being harassed while they're trying to eat.

Bear behavior is sometimes unpredictable. We can observe them and learn a lot, but we'll never be able to predict in advance what a particular animal will do in every situation.

The Great Smoky Mountains National Park attracts over nine million people a year who come to enjoy the views and learn about the flora, fauna, history, and culture of the region. The Park is one of the few remaining places of refuge for wild black bears, *Ursus americanus*, and the Park's bears are its most popular residents.

Please keep in mind when you're viewing bears that we're compromising their world. So, we need to go the extra mile not to interfere with them or endanger them.

Here are a few key points you should keep in mind when encountering a black bear. Be very careful how you manage the food you bring into the Park and the scraps and garbage you leave behind. Food that isn't secured and scraps or garbage that isn't properly disposed of cause the biggest problems in keeping bears and tourists safe and healthy.

This is how it happens—a wild bear cub is taught by its mother to stay away from people, to be afraid of them, but when they're older and mom is not around, they sometimes smell food in a picnic area at night and don't see any people around, they might take a chance and wander in to look for food scraps. Being hungry makes bears and people do some strange things.

When a bear gets food this way, it's encouraged to take bigger and bigger chances. It'll get bolder and will start to forage in the daytime and eventually things will escalate to the point that the bear is foraging in the daytime when people are around.

As you've read in the stories in this book, a bear that has lost its fear of people usually results in problems. So, when this happens, rangers try to stop the positive rewards (food and garbage) and reverse the process, if possible.

Training bears to stay away from human food is easier if they're caught in their earliest misbehaviors. A bear that starts to regularly visit a picnic area or campground at night is caught in a live capture culvert trap. Then it is immobilized with drugs, ear tagged, and tattooed for identification purposes, and has a small non-functional tooth pulled to determine how old they are. The bear is then released back in its home territory as close as possible to where it was caught.

If the unpleasant, negative memory of being captured and dominated by a human is stronger than the positive experience of getting food or scraps, the bear will usually re-develop a fear of people and won't come back to the area, at least when people are present.

Although the experience for the bear during a temporary capture may be unpleasant, it helps to protect the bear from us. In the Smokies, humans are the only black bear predator. If they're safe from us, they live longer lives.

The Great Smoky Mountain National Park covers 800 square miles, and we have approximately 1,600 bears in the Park, so that's about two bears per square mile. That's a lot of bears using the same area as our nine million tourists. This is why it's important for visitors to understand a few basic principles. If you're wondering how you should behave when you come into an area with a bear, here are some brief guidelines.

Don't get so close to the bear that you disturb its natural feeding behavior. Park regulations forbid people from intentionally approaching closer than fifty yards, or any other distance that would disturb or displace the animal.

If a bear approaches you when you're outside the Park, at a cabin for example, try to quickly secure any food you have outside, get it inside the cabin or into a vehicle, then retreat to the inside of the cabin or vehicle. Don't run away from the animal. Don't leave any garbage whatsoever out at night, not even birdseed in a feeder or a fruit rind tossed into the bushes. It's potentially the most harmful thing you can do. Remember that it's the little things that can matter.

If a bear approaches you when you are inside the Park, don't turn and run. Don't climb a tree. This might provoke a chase response, and bears are excellent at running and climbing trees. Walk away slowly. Talk to the bear in a soft voice while you are walking away, so it can tell you are leaving.

If a bear approaches you when you are in a campground, look around and see what food you have available. Try to quickly secure it inside a camper or vehicle. If you need to, try to scare the bear away. Make noise and throw things at the bear. Then report the incident to the rangers.

If a bear approaches you when you are on a hiking trail, it's important to determine the reason it's coming toward you, so you can make the appropriate response. If you encounter a bear and it swats the ground with its paws and makes huffing noises, this usually indicates a defensive behavior. The bear is telling you that you are too close. So what should you do?

You should slowly back up and give the bear some space, talking in a calm tone. If a bear persists in approaching you without vocalizing or swatting its paws, the reason for its approach is not always clear. It's possible the bear is trying to determine what you are, or it may be after your food; or, in rare cases, it may consider you as prey. This is serious.

If this happens, talk to the bear in a low tone and slowly back up. If the bear continues toward you, change your direction. If the bear is getting closer, gather your group together and stand your ground. Start talking in a very loud and authoritative voice. Make yourself and your group look as big possible. Stand on a log or rock and throw sticks and rocks as you yell. Act dominant, authoritative, and forceful. If you have bear pepper spray, this is probably a good time to use it.

Make as much noise as you can, but stand your ground. Do not run. You cannot outrun or outclimb a bear. You need to quickly establish dominance over the approaching bear.

If you think the bear is after your food—if, for example, it runs over to investigate what you've thrown at it—that usually indicates that someone has thrown food to the bear in the past and that's what it wants. If it continues toward you and makes contact with you—grabs, slaps, or bites you—quickly separate yourself from your food.

Take your backpack off and back away slowly, talking to the animal as you back up. If you don't think the bear is after your food and you're physically attacked, fight back with anything possible. Playing dead is not a good strategy when dealing with black bears in the Smokies.

When you know and do the right things, you not only help protect yourself, but also you protect the other visitors and the bears in the Great Smoky Mountains National Park.

You can get in touch with Kim by email at
BlackBearBook@gmail.com

His Facebook page is https://www.facebook.com/BlackBearBook
His Twitter address is https://twitter.com/BlackBearBook

Kim is an experienced speaker, teacher, and workshop leader.
Contact him at BlackBearBook@gmail.com if you'd like to schedule
an event.

If you'd like Kim to autograph you book, mail it, along with return
postage, to:
E. Kim DeLozier
229 South Shiloh Road
Seymour, TN 37865

DEDICATION

Kim DeLozier

This book is dedicated first and foremost to my Lord and Savior, Jesus Christ, who provides my strength and guidance each and every day. I am so thankful to him just to be born in America where at least I live in a free country and for being raised by two outstanding Christian parents, Bill and Barbara. Over thirty years ago, God also graciously blessed my life with a wonderful wife and two healthy children, and to top it off, he gave me a career that was tailor made just for me. For that, I am eternally grateful.

Without hesitation, my next line of support in my life comes from my wife and best friend, Donna. She has always been there to keep me on the straight and narrow. She was there to help me when I didn't really deserve to be helped, and love me when I didn't deserve to be loved, and listened to me when she really did not want to listen. She successfully held down the fort for our family on countless nights that I was away either camping in the backcountry or gone for an out of town meeting or event. Although she occasionally said she was scared at night, she never really seriously complained. She always asked, "Honey, when will you be home?" Donna was also the primary leader in raising our two children and raised them far better than I could have ever done alone. She was also able to keep them in order by saying, "You do that again and I promise you that I'll tell your Dad when he comes home." I appreciate her willingness and professionalism in answering the hundreds of phone calls relating to my job of managing the critters in the Park. I can still hear her now giving advice to a fearful caller that had just seen a bear, "Sir, just be sure to put your garbage inside and do not leave any dog or cat food outside. Everything will be okay then." Without Donna's support, concern, and love for me, I would not have had success in handling the demanding and sometimes stressful times in my job and for that, I am forever indebted and extremely grateful to her.

Mom died on October 23, 2007 but I feel she is still beside me every day. I especially want to dedicate this book to her for her unconditional love, never ending support and her sincere encouragement. Because she was always there to help me along, I was the first in our family to attend and graduate from college. She knew I did not like school. She always told me that I could do whatever I set my mind to do. I believed her. Along with Mom's support and encouragement was that from my Dad, Bill. We spent many days together cutting tobacco, feeding chickens, chasing cows (or them chasing us), hauling hay, or fixing a fence. I appreciate him for giving me the opportunity to grow up and work on the family farm. The values he instilled in me will stay with me forever. His conservative financial guidance and mentoring is still alive and well in me today; just ask my family. Mom and Dad, thanks for all you did in providing me a life that anyone would be proud of and fortunate to have.

I also dedicate this book to my children, Carrie and Travis, and their wonderful families. I appreciate them for the life decisions they have made and continue to make as they grow older. They lived through the years when I was gone because of work related things. Travis is just a chip off the ole block, but a much better one. I do want to say that I'm sorry to him for scarring him for life by intentionally scaring him when around a bear, wild hog, or snake. Maybe he will get over it, but I doubt it. Travis is a great Dad to his two boys and a person I feel fortunate to call my son. I appreciate Carrie for being a great mother to her two boys and for being such a good friend to so many. I could not ask for a better daughter. I'm also thankful for her letting me win a few friendly arguments between us. She was always better. Seriously, I am so proud of my kids and their families. I love them, appreciate them and am very, very proud to call them my family. They are surely one of my biggest blessings in life.

I'd also like to dedicate this book to all those co-workers, supervisors, and employees that gave of themselves to ensure that wild animals in the Smokies have a home forever. All the many calls after hours, the late work schedules, working on weekends and holidays, the call-ins are all reminders of the kind of top notch professionals I was fortunate to work with. The constant dedication, concern, and devotion shown are why wildlife in the Park is well today. Although the list of all the people that supported and helped me is too long to mention, I do want to give a special thanks to Bill Stiver, Joe Yarkovich, Carroll Schell, Joe Abrell, Stu Coleman, Bill Cook, Buck Branam, Rick Varner, Chuck Hester, Blake McCann, Jay Clark, Jennifer Murrow, Steve Dobey, Dale Raxter, Terry Esker, Bob Koerkenmeier, Dr. Joe Clark, Dr. Mike Pelton and Dan Nolfi. Also, kudos goes out to Dr. John New and Dr. Ed Ramsay from the University of Tennessee for their unending guidance, superior knowledge, and invaluable veterinarian expertise in caring for the health of our critters. Dr. New's unexpected passing in 2013 left a deep void in our hearts. Many thanks to Tom Toman with the Rocky Mountain Elk Foundation, Terry Maddox and Steve Kemp with the Great Smoky Mountains Association and President Jim Hart and former President Charles Maynard with Friends of the Smokies (FOTS). A very special and sincere thanks goes to Tennessee Supreme Court Chief Justice Gary Wade who has been a good friend and support for me throughout my career. Also, thanks to all those from Appalachian Bear Rescue for giving many unfortunate bears a second chance to return to the wild. The bears thank you, too.

Finally, I want thank many of those not directly associated with the Park that supported me and helped so much to further the Park's wildlife programs, especially with returning elk to the Smokies. Some, but definitely not all, are Joyce Cooper, Ray and Ramona Bryson, Arnold Bryson, Tim Queen, Joe Treadway, David Shiflett, Dwight Flynn, Jerry and Ramona King, John Mechler, Lee Gamble, Barry Holbert, Mike Stiles, Wayne Edge, Bob Hunter, Bill Farmer, David Ensley, Cherokee Chief Michell Hicks, Vice-Chief Larry Blythe, Former Chief Leon Jones (deceased), John "Thunder" Thornton, Mike Carraway, Forrest Parker, Courtney Lix, and last, but definitely not least, is Bobby Boyd.

I owe my life, career, and accomplishments to so many. I pray God would graciously bless them every day of their lives. If wild animals in the Smoky Mountains could talk, I know they would thank them too.

Carolyn Jourdan

This book is dedicated with deep respect, admiration, and affection to the wildlife rangers in the Great Smoky Mountains National Park.

Although they wear their heroism with great modesty, these rangers risk their lives on a routine basis to protect the more than nine million people who visit the Great Smoky Mountains National Park every year, as well as each other, and the bears, elk, and other wildlife in the Park.

And also to my parents, Paul L. Jourdan, M.D. and Elise G. Jourdan, Pharm. D., and my brother, David C. Jourdan.